Telling God's Story

Year Two Activity Book: The Kingdom of Heaven

Student Guide and Activity Pages

Edited by Justin Moore

With Activities and Illustrations by
Stacy Bartholomew, Chris Bauer, Mollie Bauer, Sara Buffington,
Alia Macrina Heise, Justin Moore, Sarah Park, Jeff West,
and Madelaine Wheeler

Olive Branch Books
Charles City, Virginia

ISBN 978-1-933339-51-1

This book is to be used in conjunction with *Telling God's Story, Year Two Instructor Text and Teaching Guide*; ISBN 978-1-933339-50-4

Photocopying and Distribution Policy
Extra copies of the student pages and coloring pages are available as a PDF download at www.peacehillpress.com.

For families: you may make as many photocopies of the student pages as you need for use WITHIN YOUR OWN FAMILY ONLY. Photocopying the pages so that the book can then be resold is a violation of copyright.

Schools, co-ops, and churches MAY NOT PHOTOCOPY any portion of this Activity Guide. Smaller schools sometimes find that purchasing a set of the pre-copied student pages for each student is the best option. Or you may purchase a classroom license ($100 per volume, per year) that allows duplication for school, church, or co-op use. For more information, please contact our parent company, Peace Hill Press: email info@peacehillpress.com; phone 1.877.322.3445.

Art Credits/Permissions:
Page 23: National Gallery, London/Art Resource, NY

Table of Contents

Using This Student Guide

This Student Guide is designed to accompany *Telling God's Story: Year Two Instructor Text and Teaching Guide*, by Peter Enns (ISBN 978-1-933339-50-4). It expands on the lessons in that book, providing coloring pages, projects, games, and memory work. Some of these activities provide opportunities to put the lessons into practice; others help the student experience the customs, geography, clothing, or culture of the New Testament world; still others reveal the ways in which artists in different eras have depicted biblical stories. For each lesson in the *Instructor Text*, this *Student Guide* contains at least two activities (sometimes three or four), and a coloring page. In addition, a series of Memory Work activities runs throughout the entire year; by the end of the school year the student will have reviewed the material memorized in Year One (the twelve disciples and the books of the New Testament) and will also have memorized several important passages from the Old and New Testaments.

The directions for each activity contain a list of the necessary materials, but you will also find a comprehensive list of materials on page xi–xiii.

A Typical Week in This Curriculum

Aim to complete one lesson per week. Each lesson in the *Instructor Text* opens with a brief word of explanation to the parent; this will help you in helping your children process the content of the lessons. You should spend a few moments reading the parent section ("What the Parent Should Know") from the *Instructor Text* the night before the lesson so you can ponder a bit; or if you prefer, read it right before the lesson so it is fresh in your mind—whatever works for you. The important thing is that you spend some time becoming familiar with the information so you can be of more help to your children. The purpose of these parent sections is to orient you to the biblical passage for that day. The parent sections are more detailed and complex than the scripted lessons; this will give you a broader handle on the issues surrounding the passage. It will also give you a greater vantage point from which to look at the lesson itself and, perhaps, to address questions that might come up.

Next, you may wish to read the scripted lesson from the *Instructor Text* to the student on the first day as he or she colors the coloring page for that lesson in the *Activity Book*, and then to complete projects on the second and third days. Alternately, you may read the scripted lesson on the first day, complete the coloring page on the second, and complete a chosen project on the third.

In a group setting that meets once a week, plan to read the scripted lesson as the students color and then to conclude the day's study with one of the projects or games especially suited for group or classroom use (see the list of these projects on page xv–xvi).

Photocopying and Distribution Policy

Additional copies of the student pages (coloring pages, mazes, craft templates, etc) are available as PDF downloads. To purchase them, visit our website, www.olivebranchbooks.net, click on "Buy the Books," and look for "Year Two Activity Guide Student Pages."

For families: you may make as many photocopies of the student pages as you need for use WITHIN YOUR OWN FAMILY ONLY. Photocopying the pages so that the book can then be resold is a violation of copyright.

Schools, co-ops, and churches MAY NOT PHOTOCOPY any portion of this Activity Guide. Smaller schools sometimes find that purchasing a set of the pre-copied student pages for each student is the best option. Or you may purchase a classroom license ($100 per volume, per year) that allows duplication for school, church, and co-op use. For more information, please contact Peace Hill Press: email info@peacehillpress.com; phone 1.877.322.3445.

Materials List

This materials list includes craft and unusual items that may need to be acquired ahead of time. It does not include ingredients for recipes, items which are very likely to be found around the house, or the following school supplies, which are used multiple times and should be on hand: construction paper, school glue, tape, scissors, crayons, colored pencils.

Acrylic paint, black	34
Active dry yeast, ¼ tsp.	30
Adhesive bandage, small	3
Aluminum foil	6, 29, 33
Alum powder, ⅓ cup	Supplemental Lesson 1
Baking pan with raised sides	24
Baking sheet	5, 21, 34
Bandanna	10
Bible	10, 34
Bleach gel pen	20
Blindfold	7, 15, 18
Bricks or Blocks (4)	12
Bucket or gallon container, one per student	12
Buttons	6
Cardboard	3, 6, 20, 21, 33
Casserole dishes (one 9"x13" and one 8"x11")	25, 29
Citrus rinds	Supplemental Lesson 2
Cheesecloth	15, Supplemental Lesson 2
Clear tape	6
Corn husks (15)	10
Cornmeal	30
Costume clothing (see Materials List in lesson)	5
Craft foam, 2 sheets	14
Craft paint in brown, white, tan, or black (choose one or more colors)	16 (optional)
Dice	3
Dowels (2) (10" long, ⅓" diameter), or 2 sticks of similar dimensions	29
Dry, uncooked split peas or uncooked rice, 1½ cups	6
Dye source, 7 oz. (see Materials List in lesson for options)	Supplemental Lesson 1
Embroidery floss	6
Felt	6
Flour	30 (6 cups), 34
Fresh berries like strawberries, blueberries, or raspberries	Supplemental Lesson 2

Group/Classroom Activities

These activities are particularly suited to group or classroom settings, though many of the others would be appropriate as well. In addition, every lesson in this book contains a coloring page for students to color.

Lesson 1: Make a Vineyard, Grape Pop Code
Lesson 2: Grow "The Kingdom of God" Grass, Seed Experiment, See the Kingdom that is Growing
Lesson 3: Picture Study of *The Good Samaritan*, The Good Samaritan Board Game, Neighbor Tangle
Lesson 4: Learn the Trisagion Hymn with Hand Motions, "How Many Times Should We Forgive?" Word Search, Memory Work
Lesson 5: Frozen Grapes, *The Laborers in the Vineyard* Play, Memory Work
Lesson 6: Make a "Herod's Temple" Coin Bank and a Shekel, Giving Back, Coin, Coin, Who's Got the Coin?
Lesson 7: Crossword Puzzle of Jesus' Miracles, Trust Game
Lesson 8: Remembering to Be Thankful
Lesson 9: Learn a Finger-Play and Poem, Outsider Tag
Lesson 10: Map Activity: Important Places in the Life of Jesus
Lesson 11: Musical Chairs With a Twist
Lesson 12: Eat an Ancient Snack on the Floor, Burden Tag
Lesson 13: Defend the Sheep!, Shepherd's Belt, Memory Work
Lesson 14: "I Belong to Jesus" Photo Frame, Memory Work
Lesson 15: Nature Hike: The Life of Trees, Make Your Own Grape Juice, Stay Connected to the Vine
Lesson 16: Blow a Shofar Horn to Announce Your Good Deeds
Lesson 17: Science Activity: Earthly Treasure Doesn't Last, Serving Two Masters Game
Lesson 18: What Do I Have?
Lesson 19: "Broad and Narrow Paths" Maze
Lesson 20: Good Tree Board Game, Design a "Good Trees" T-Shirt
Lesson 21: Make a High Priest's Breastplate, Take a Vow of Silence, "The Angel's Announcement" Word Search
Lesson 22: Waiting for the King
Lesson 23: Make an Illuminated *Magnificat*, Memory Work
Lesson 24: Create Names On A Writing Tablet, Anthroponomastics, Memory Work
Lesson 25: Boat Maze
Lesson 26: Humility Crossword Puzzle
Lesson 27: Acts of Kindness in Jesus' Name, Names of God Around the World

Materials for Group/Classroom Activities

This materials list includes craft and unusual items that may need to be acquired ahead of time. It does not include ingredients for recipes, items which the students' parents are likely to have on hand, or the following common school supplies which are used multiple times and should be on hand: construction paper, tape, scissors, pencils, crayons, and glue sticks. You will also need copies of the workbook pages for each student. For copying and licensing information, see the copyright page of this book.

Acrylic paint, black	34
Adhesive bandage, small	3
Aluminum foil	33
Baking pan with raised sides	24
Baking sheet	5, 21
Bible	10, 36, Supplemental Lesson 3
Bleach gel pen	20
Blindfold	7, 15, 18
Bowl	12, 33
Bricks or Blocks (4)	12
Bucket or gallon container, one per student	12
Cardboard	3, 6, 20, 21, 33
Cheesecloth	15
Cinnamon, ground	31
Cloth, large	12
Coins (nickels, dimes and quarters)	3, 5, 6, 17
Colored candies, a different colored piece per player	20
Costume clothing (see Materials List in lesson)	5
Craft paint in brown, white, tan, or black (choose one or more colors)	16 (optional)
Cushion, comfortable	11
Dice	3
Drinking glasses	15
Flashlight	Supplemental Lesson 1
Freezer space	5
Grapes	1, 5, 15
Grape vines or other type of vine	1
Grass seed, handful	2
Hammer	32
Hand soap	31
Highlighter marker	5, 24

Unit 1

Stories Jesus Told

Lesson 1: Talking the Talk & Walking the Walk

Activities

Activity: **Disobedient or Obedient?**
Craft Project: **Make a "Vineyard"**
Game (Group or Individual): **Grape Pop Code**
Coloring Page: **The Obedient Son and the Disobedient Son**

Activity

· ·

Disobedient or Obedient?

This activity shows the different ways you can respond to requests and commands.

Directions

1   Pick an activity or job you can do with the student. We will use getting dinner ready as an example, but you could also ask the student to clean up or organize various things in his room, sort or fold laundry, do something on her chore list, etc.

2   <u>Be a Child Who Says Yes But Does Nothing</u>: Ask the student to do various tasks like "Put plates on the table," "Add the tomatoes to the salad," and "Fold up the napkins." Let the student come up with over-the-top ways to say she will obey: "I would love to!" or "Right away!" or "Yes! Yes!" or "Nothing would make me happier than to do what you ask!" No matter what the student says, she should not do <u>anything</u> to help. Do this five or six times (or more, if you are having fun).

3   <u>Be a Child Who Says No But Then Obeys</u>: Ask the student to do more tasks and have her come up with funny ways to refuse you: "No way I'm doing that!" or "I'm too busy resting," or "You've got to be kidding!" The student should wait a moment after her refusal, and then obey the command anyway.

4   Switch roles with the student. Have *her* ask *you* to do a few things. First, be one who says yes and does nothing, and then be someone who says no but changes his mind and obeys.

5   Discuss with the student, "What kind of person would you rather have helping you: one who only promises to obey you or one who actually does obey you?"

6   Finish the activity by being both willing and obedient. Ask the student to do something for you. She should respond enthusiastically (for example, saying "Absolutely!") and then quickly finish the task.

Make a "Vineyard"

Materials

- Large piece of thick paper or poster board cut in half
- Poster paint in green, blue and brown
- Paintbrushes
- Glue, or hot glue
- Popsicle sticks
- Thin grape vines or other type of vine (available at craft stores or found outside easily in some areas)
- Plastic leaves (in the silk flower section at craft store)
- Something to represent grapes (paint, plastic grapes from the store, raisins . . .)

Directions

1   Have the student paint a background for your vineyard on the thick paper or posterboard using the green, blue, and brown paint. She may want to include a field, some rolling hills and a blue sky. Let the paint dry.

2   Use the Popsicle sticks to make the trellis for your grapevines. (Explain to the student that the trellis is a wooden structure that helps the grapevines stay up.) Stack two Popsicle sticks on top of each other for height on either side of the paper and stack two in the middle. Lay the other popsicle sticks diagonally to make a criss-cross pattern, or horizontally and vertically to create a fence post pattern. See the diagram below.

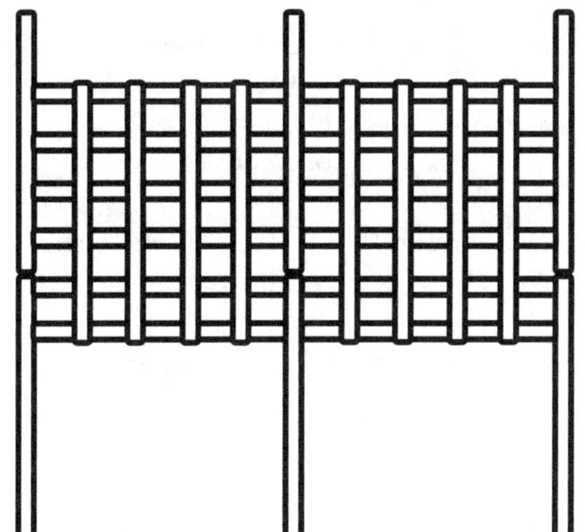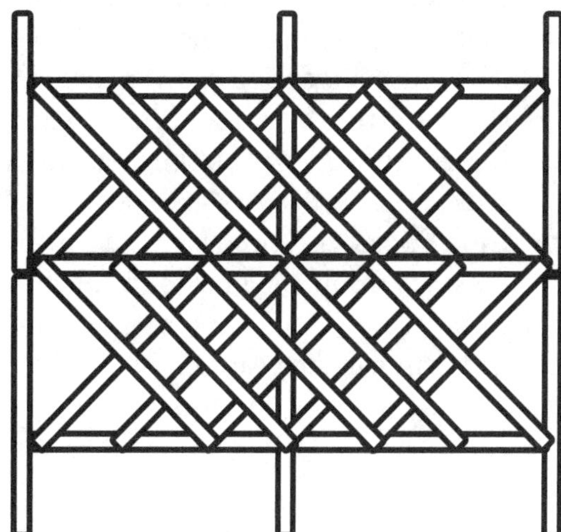

3   Then glue your vines on—hot glue may be needed—or just allow plenty of drying time. Next add some leaves.

4   Finally add your grapes; either paint them on adjacent to the vines and leaves or glue on your three-dimensional grapes.

Grape Pop Code

Make a pattern with grapes to reveal a hidden—and edible—message. When choosing the bags of grapes at the store, try to pick green and purple grapes that are about the same size. This project can be done by an individual student—she will just have plenty of grapes to eat (or freeze for later). If you have more than seventeen students (fewer is fine), then you will need to double this activity and do it in two sections.

Materials

- Grape Code Hidden Message (Student Page 7); Best to have 1 copy for each student
- 17 wooden skewers or long lollipop sticks (available at craft stores)
- Masking tape
- Marker
- 38 purple grapes of similar size, stems removed and rinsed
- 47 green grapes of similar size, stems removed and rinsed

Directions

1   Before class, tear off a piece of masking tape and fold it around the base (dull end) of each lollipop stick or skewer to make a little flag. Use the marker and write a number on each flag, 1 through 17.
2   Divide the sticks among the members of the class.
3   Look at the Grape Code Hidden Message Sheet. Distribute the code for the stick whose number is on the flag. Each student needs to skewer the grapes in order, starting from the bottom (flagged) end and going up, so that the stick the student makes matches the order on the Grape Code Hidden Message Sheets.
4   Pierce each grape at the grape "hole" where the stem was attached. (This is not an issue if you use a wooden skewer since the tip is sharp. You should snip the tip off the wooden skewer after the student has threaded the grapes. This will make for safer eating later!)
5   Once the student has finished threading each stick, set it aside. Complete the remaining sticks.
6   Line Sticks 1–17 in order, side-by-side with no space between them. Read the hidden message in purple grapes to solve the puzzle. Answer: "Jesus wants followers who **OBEY** him."
7   You can eat the grapes now or place them in a single layer inside a freezer bag and freeze overnight. Now you have frozen grape pops.

Answer Key:

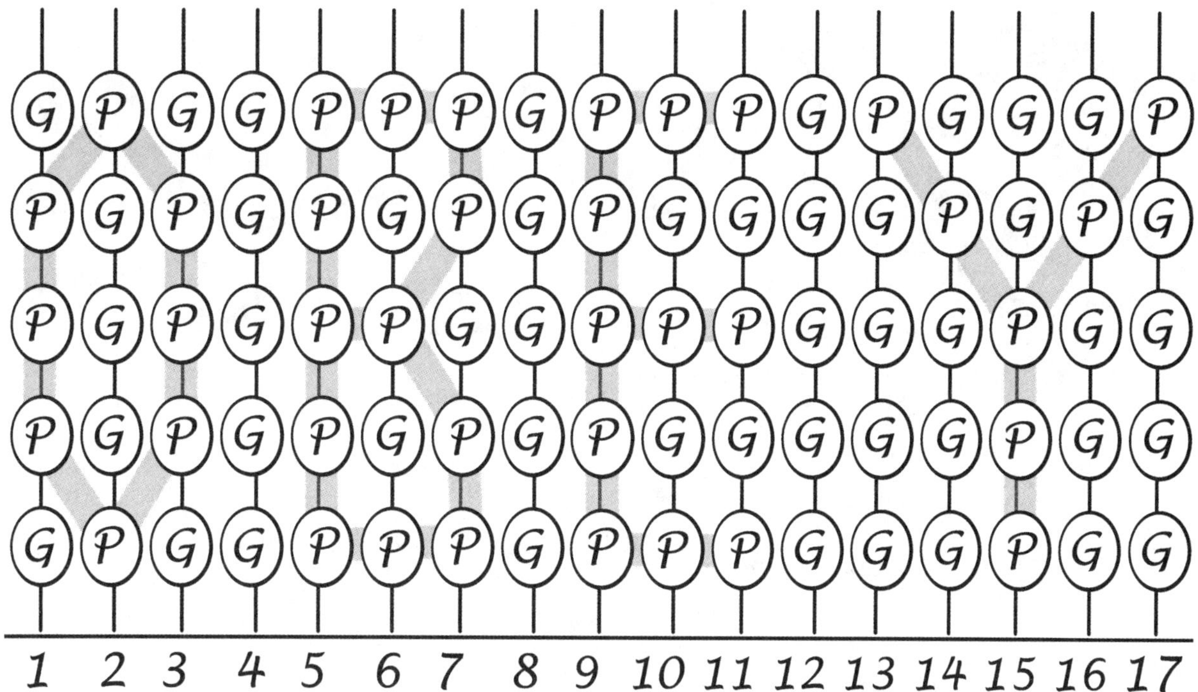

Coloring Page

The Obedient Son and the Disobedient Son

Jesus' parable tells of a son who said he would obey, but then did not, and of a son who didn't say he would obey, but then did. Doing what Jesus says is better than just *saying* we'll do what Jesus says.

Grape Code Hidden Message Sheet

Thread the grapes in the order below to reveal the hidden answer.

G= green grape, P= purple grape

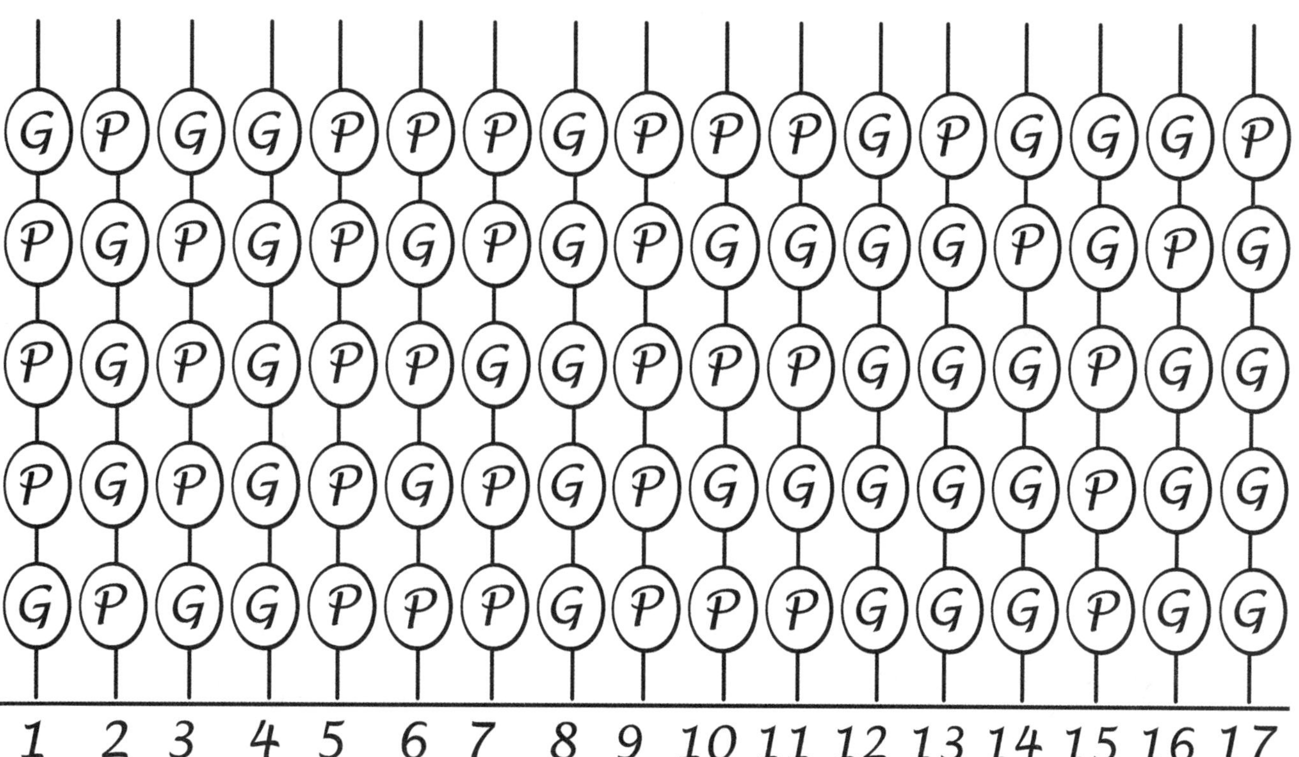

SECRET MESSAGE:

Jesus wants followers who ________________ him.

Matthew 21:28–32
The Obedient Son and the Disobedient Son

Lesson 2: The Kingdom of God Grows on its Own

Activities

Science Activity: **Grow "The Kingdom of God" Grass**
Craft Project: **See the Kingdom that is Growing**
Science Activity: **Seed Experiment**
Coloring Page: **The Kingdom Grows**

Science Project

• •

Grow "The Kingdom of God" Grass

Here is a plant that grows on its own with minimal tending from you. Keep this plant in a windowsill to remind the family that the Kingdom of God is hardy and resilient. If you are making the plant in a class, make the nylon ball and send it home with instructions on how to grow the grass.

Materials (for each student)

- 4 craft sticks
- Glue
- Clear plastic cup
- 1 knee-high nude pantyhose
- Handful of grass seed (available at many home & garden stores or hardware stores)
- 1 cup of potting mix (available at many home & garden stores or hardware stores)
- Scissors
- Black permanent marker
- Growth Instructions (Student Page 15)

Directions

1. Have the student arrange the craft sticks to make a pattern like a tic-tac-toe board (two horizontal sticks intersecting two vertical sticks). Glue in place. Set aside on top of the cup to dry.
2. Give the student the pantyhose and have him put a handful of grass seed at the bottom. Next add the cup of dirt. DO NOT MIX! The idea is to layer them.

3   Have the student knot the pantyhose right above the dirt to create a firm ball.

4   Turn the ball upside down so the "tail" hangs down. Trim the tail with the scissors so that it is just a bit longer than the height of the plastic cup.

5   Keeping the ball so the tail hangs down, have the student write "The Kingdom of God" with the Black Sharpie around the sides of the cup.

6   Send the nylon ball, cup, craft sticks, and Growth Instructions home with the student (see step 7 for a copy of these instructions). Go over the growth instructions with the student before class ends.

7   Growth Instructions: 1. Fill the cup halfway with water. Submerge the nylon ball and let it soak in the water overnight. 2. Then remove the ball and fill the cup with water three-quarters full. Set the craft stick grid on top of the cup. Thread the tail of the ball through the center of the grid so that it dangles in the water (this acts as a wick to draw up the water). Let the ball rest on top of the grid. 3. Now leave it alone. Just check on it once in a while to refill the water as necessary. It may take a week or so to sprout, depending on the variety of grass you used, but once it does you will have a vibrant plant that requires very little tending!

Craft Project

See the Kingdom that is Growing

Materials

- Map of the world
- Computer with Internet access

Directions

1   Say to the student, "In this week's lesson we learned about God's kingdom that Jesus began. It has been growing ever since. The lesson said, 'All over the world are people who love God and follow Jesus every day.' We are going to learn more about some of those people."

2   Help the student check out one of the following websites, and choose one project to do together this week:

- www.kidsonmission.org provides videos of Christian children around the world, downloadable resources, maps to print and color, prayer requests, information on other cultures, and more.
- www.biblesunbound.com helps provide Bibles in many languages to Christians around the world. Use the world map to look up the countries mentioned. Your student might collect loose change to save up, and donate the proceeds toward purchasing a Bible in another language for a Christian in another country.
- www.operationworld.org provides information on Christians in every country in the world, and gives frequently-updated suggestions for praying for those countries. The site features clickable maps that you and your student can navigate together. Your student, after learning about a particular country, might pray for that country and its people today. The organization also publishes books for children: *You Can Change the World*, and *You Can Change the World, Volume 2.*

Seed Experiment

Materials

- Two small potting containers
- Potting soil
- Outside dirt (somewhat sandy is a plus)
- Seeds of the same variety (Runner beans work well because they sprout quickly; nasturtiums are also a good choice. Available at www.parkseed.com and at garden stores)

Directions

1 Label one pot "Neglected Seeds" and label one pot "Cared-for Seeds."
2 Plant seeds in two different potting containers. Plant one in potting soil and the other in the sandy dirt from outside. Place the set of beans in the potting soil at a proper depth. Plant the other ones more shallowly.
3 Slightly moisten the neglected seeds; properly moisten the cared-for seeds. Place the neglected seeds in a location with not much sunlight and place the cared-for seeds in a place with adequate sunlight. Don't moisten the dirt on the neglected seeds at all, but care well for the other seeds. Check the cared-for seeds every day, and have the student add a bit of water to the soil if it feels dry.
4 Examine the seeds after a week, and see if there's been any progress. Ask the student, "Did the cared-for seeds do better than the neglected seeds?" Say, "Normally, you have to pay attention to seeds and water them and plant them just right, for them to grow. It's easy for them to stop growing. But nothing can stop God's kingdom from growing, all the time."

Coloring Page

The Kingdom Grows

Jesus said that God's kingdom is like the wheat in this wheatfield, which grows night and day until it is huge.

"The Kingdom of God Grass"
Growth Instructions

TO GROW THE PLANT:
Fill the cup halfway with water. Submerge the nylon ball and let it soak in the water overnight.

The next morning, remove the ball and fill the cup with water three-quarters full. Set the craft stick grid on top of the cup. Thread the tail of the ball through the center of the grid so that it dangles in the water (this acts as a wick to draw up the water). Let the ball rest on top of the grid.

Now leave it alone! Just check on it once in a while to refill the water as necessary. It may take a week or so to sprout, depending on the variety of grass you used, but once it does you will have a vibrant plant that requires very little tending. Just like it says in the lesson, the kingdom of God grows like a seed that "does not need to be watered and fed. This seed grows no matter what. Wherever Jesus went and talked about God, people kept coming from all over to listen to Jesus. The kingdom of God got getting bigger and bigger. Nothing could stop it."

Mark 4:26–29
The Kingdom Grows

Lesson 3: Everyone is Your Neighbor

Activities

Art History Activity: **Picture Study of *The Good Samaritan***
Put It Into Practice Activity: **Be a Good Neighbor**
Game: **The Good Samaritan Board Game**
Group Game: **Neighbor Tangle**
Coloring Page: **The Good Samaritan Helps a Man in Trouble**

Art History Activity

. . . .

Picture Study of *The Good Samaritan*

The Good Samaritan is one of Jesus' most famous parables, and many artists have created portrayals of it. Today your student will learn about one of these.

Materials

- Copy of *The Good Samaritan* by Jacopo Bassano (Student Page 23)

Directions

1. First, tell the student something about the artist and the painting. Say to the Student, "This painting was done by Jacopo Bassano, who lived almost five hundred years ago. He lived in Italy. His father, a painter, taught him how to paint, and later Jacopo taught his sons to paint too. He painted many pictures of stories from the Bible."
2. Tear out the picture of Bassano's *The Good Samaritan* on Student Page 23.
3. Say "Look at Jacopo Bassano's painting, *The Good Samaritan.*" Give the student some time to look at the picture. A color version can be seen online at http://www.nationalgallery.org.uk/paintings/jacopo-bassano-the-good-samaritan.
4. Say, "Now I will ask you some questions. Try to answer in complete sentences. Think about the story from the lesson. Now look at the painting. What is happening in this painting?" (The good Samaritan is taking care of the hurt man.)

   How did the man get hurt? (Robbers attacked him)
   Why do you think the man isn't wearing many clothes? (The robbers took them.)

Who are the other two men in the background of the painting? (They are the priest and the Levite who would not stop to help the hurt man.)

What do you think the building is that is far behind the Samaritan? (That is the inn)

What will happen next? (The Samaritan will take the hurt man to the inn and make sure he is taken care of.)

Be a Good Neighbor

While opportunities to help dying robbery-victims, such as the man in this lesson, are rare, even young students can begin to practice a mindset of generous service.

Directions

1   Pick a time in which you and the student will be doing errands together. Say to the student, "In this week's Bible lesson, Jesus said that his followers should go out of their way to be kind to others. We probably won't see an injured person who's been beaten up by robbers, like the man in the story, but we can look for people who might need our help."

2   Throughout the whole trip, look for opportunities to be a "Good Samaritan." Here are some suggestions:

- Help or accompany an elderly person into the store
- Ask your neighbor if there is anything you can do for him or her during your errands (drop off a library book, pick up mail or an item at the store, perform yard chores, etc).
- Reach something off the shelf for someone having trouble reaching
- Hold the door for the person behind you
- Pay for the person's coffee in the drive-through line behind you
- Carry bags to someone's car for them
- Alert store staff to a spill that nobody has taken care of
- If you see an item out of place, put it back in its proper location

3   Keep track of how many people you helped in that one trip.

The Good Samaritan Board Game

Materials

- Old magazines
- Scissors (child-size and adult-size)
- Good Samaritan Game Board (Student Page 25)
- Good Samaritan Playing Card Template (Student Page 27)
- Markers, colored pencils, or crayons (including a thick, black, permanent marker)
- Thin cardboard (such as from a cereal box), 10"x7"

- Craft glue or a glue stick
- Photograph of the student, roughly 2" x 2.5"
- One small adhesive bandage
- Two balls of modeling clay or play-dough, roughly 1.5" in diameter
- Two nickels
- Two dice
- Timer

Directions for Making the Game Pieces

1   Help the student look through the magazines to find photographs of people who look different from her, whether in age, gender, race, economic status, etc. Choose five pictures. Using the permanent marker, the teacher should draw a roughly 2" x 2.5" box around the chosen photos. The student may then cut them out.
2   Instruct the student to tear out the game board page (Student Page 25). Have her cut out the outer rectangle (thick border) of the Good Samaritan Playing Card Template (Student Page 27), but DO NOT cut apart the smaller rectangles (thin lines). She may color the game board as desired.
3   Meanwhile, the instructor should trace the full sheet of the Good Samaritan Playing Card Template onto the cardboard, and then cut the cardboard.
4   Help the student to glue the Good Samaritan Playing Card Template onto the cardboard. Then cut out the individual playing cards.
5   Instruct the student to glue the photographs from step one, as well as her own, onto the individual playing cards. Allow to dry.
6   Take the piece of cardboard with the student's photograph on it, and push it gently into one of the balls of modeling clay, so that it can stand up and be a game piece to move around the board.

Playing Instructions

1   Set up the game: Place the shuffled playing cards in a stack, with the photograph faces facing down. Place the student's game piece at the "Start." Take the two nickels, and push them into the same ball of modeling clay, on either side of the student's photo card.
2   The student may now roll the dice, and move her game piece accordingly.
3   Once she has landed on a square with a cross, it is time to draw the top card from the deck of playing cards. Say, "Oh no! This person is badly hurt and needs help. Find the band-aid and put it on the back of his card!"
4   The student should take the adhesive bandage, and apply it to the back of the playing card. Then help the student to put the playing card in the other ball of modeling clay, so that it can stand up, too.
5   Say, "It's time to take this person to the inn! But they can't walk well, so the going will be slow. This time when you roll the dice, you'll move your piece according to how many dots are on the higher-numbered die, and you'll move his piece according to how many dots are on the lower-numbered die. This way you will lead him to the Inn. But it's important to get him help quickly, so we have to move as fast as we can."
6   Start the timer, and proceed with the game until both players have reached the Inn. Remove the playing piece of the "injured" person, and put it on top of the Inn drawing, with the two quarters. Stop the timer. Record your time, and then, if desired, play again—trying to get a faster time.

Neighbor Tangle

This game is best played with five or more students.

Directions

1 Gather a group of students (at least five of them). Have them stand in a circle.
2 Say to the students, "In this week's lesson we learned that anyone who needs help is our neighbor. Today we're going to play a game where you'll have to help your neighbors in this class. Each of you, reach out one hand and hold hands with someone else across the circle from you . . . but it can't be the person right next to you."
3 When each student is holding the hand of one other student, say, "Good! Now, keep holding on to that hand, but reach out your OTHER hand and use it to hold hands with a different person." When this process is complete, each student should be holding hands with two other students.
4 Say to the students, "Now that you are all tangled up together, you must work together to figure out how to untangle yourselves without letting go of your neighbors' hands. When everyone is untangled, you will find that you form a giant circle." The students may need to go behind, duck under, or step over each other's arms.

The Good Samaritan Helps a Man in Trouble

This man is helping someone who was beaten up by robbers, even though the two men are from tribes that don't like each other. God wants us to be a good neighbor to all people—even the ones we don't like.

The Good Samaritan by Jacopo Bassano

Good Samaritan Game Board

Good Samaritan Playing Card Template

Luke 10:30–37
The Good Samaritan Helps a Man in Trouble

Lesson 4:
Don't Stop Forgiving Others

Activities

Music Activity: **Learn the Trisagion Hymn with Hand Motions**
Review Activity: **"How Many Times Should We Forgive?" Word Search**
Memory Work: **Review the Books of the New Testament, Part I**
Coloring Page: **The Unforgiving Servant**

Music Activity

. . . .

Learn the Trisagion Hymn with Hand Motions

Learn this ancient Christian hymn about God's mercy toward us, and learn the sign language to accompany the lyrics.

Materials

- Sign Language for the Trisagion Hymn (Student Page 35)

Directions

1   Say to the student, "God forgives us and is kind to us. We call this 'mercy.' We are going to learn a very, very old song that Christians in many parts of the world have sung, and still sing today. It's called the Trisagion. [Say 'try-SAY-gee-on.'] Let's say that name together: *try-SAY-gee-on.* That means 'thrice holy,' and it's a way of saying that God is very, very, very holy. God is perfect in every way. Asking God for his mercy and forgiveness, as this prayer does, helps us remember to show mercy and forgive other people too."

2   Over the years, Christians have written hundreds of tunes for this hymn. Your church may have one in its hymnal. Hear different versions of this hymn by searching for "Trisagion hymn English" on YouTube. Many versions in the original Greek can also be found online.

3   Teach the student the lyrics of the song: "Holy God, Holy Mighty, Holy Immortal, have mercy on us." If the student asks, explain that "immortal" means that God has been around forever and will always be around.

4   Tear out Student Pages 35-36, the Sign Language for the Trisagion Hymn.

5 Now teach the student some (slightly simplified) sign language for the words of the song. Use the drawings on the Student Page to help you, as well as the following verbal directions. If you need to see them in motion, see the video posted at <u>www.olivebranchbooks.net/trisagionvideo.html</u>

> **Holy:** hold your left hand out in front of you, palm facing you. Point the index and middle fingers of your right hand together; use the thumb to hold the other two fingers down. With the backs of the fingers facing the flat hand, sweep them across the palm of your flat hand, starting at the heel of the hand and going past the fingertips.
>
> **God:** take your left hand, fingers together, flat, with your thumb closest to you (like you were about to do a "karate chop"). In one motion, bring the hand up higher than your head and then straight down in front of you.
>
> **Mighty:** make both hands into fists, knuckles down and thumbs up, and shake your fists in front of you a little bit.
>
> **Immortal:** the left hand faces away from you, with thumb and pinkie extended out to the sides. Sweep the hand up and then again higher, in quick succession.
>
> **Have:** put thumbs of both hands up and curve fingers into a C-shape, and, with thumbs on top, start six inches from your chest and then move them toward yourself until the fingertips reach your chest.
>
> **Mercy:** Hold both hands up and away from you, with palms toward you, and bring them swooping down toward you in three looping motions. (It may help to picture "mercy descending on you from heaven.")
>
> **On:** put your left hand out, flat, palm facing down to the ground. Flatten your other hand and bring it down to rest across the back of your flattened left hand.
>
> **Me:** point to yourself with your index finger.

6 Now practice signing the prayer/hymn along with the music. Help the student to remember to practice saying the prayer before bed.

Review Activity

• •

"How Many Times Should We Forgive?" Word Search

Materials

- Pencil
- Forgiveness Word Search (Student Page 37)

Directions

1 Instruct the student to find the following words in the word search:
> Debt
> Patient
> Seven
> Denarii
> Pay
> Sin

Heart
Pity
Sold
Mercy
Servant
Talent

2 After the student has circled all the words, instruct him to color over them carefully with
   a bright crayon. Then ask him to find the remaining, uncolored letters, and fill them into
   the spaces below to discover the lesson that Jesus taught Peter.

3 Give the student help if necessary. When all the words have been found, the unused letters should form the words *Never stop forgiving.*

Memory Work

. . . .

Review the Books of the New Testament, Part I

Directions

*Note: this memory work builds on memorization that was laid out in Year One of this curriculum.
If the student didn't memorize these books last year, he may memorize them this year by taking each
segment of the following directions as an entire week's memory work.*

1 Say to the student, "Last year you learned all of the books of the New Testament.
   Remember, the New Testament is the part of the Bible that was written to tell people
   about Jesus, after he came back from the dead. It is made up of 27 little books. All the
   stories about Jesus that you're learning this year come from the New Testament. Today
   we're going to review the names of the books to keep them in your memory. The first five
   were Matthew, Mark, Luke, John, and Acts. Let's say those together twice."
   [Together, twice]: Matthew, Mark, Luke, John, Acts.

2 Then we learned nine more books, the letters that Paul wrote to different groups of
   people. They were: Romans, First and Second Corinthians, Galatians, Ephesians, Philippians, Colossians, First and Second Thessalonians. Let's say those together, twice:
   *[Say together, twice] Romans, First and Second Corinthians, Galatians, Ephesians, Philippi-
   ans, Colossians, First and Second Thessalonians.*

3 Good; you remember all of those. We're halfway through the New Testament. Let's say
   the names of all those first books again.
   *[Say together]: Matthew, Mark, Luke, John, Acts, Romans, First and Second Corinthians,
   Galatians, Ephesians, Philippians, Colossians, First and Second Thessalonians.*

The Unforgiving Servant

This man had just been forgiven for a huge amount of money that he owed. But he didn't show the same forgiveness to a man who owed him a small amount. He demanded to get all his money right now. Jesus said that we should forgive others like God forgives us.

"Holy
God,
"Holy
Mighty,

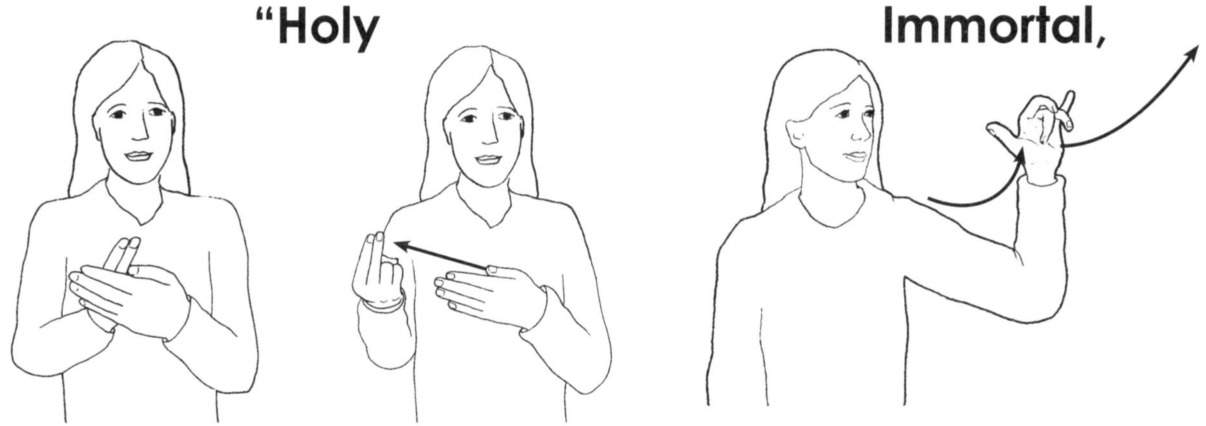

"Holy
Immortal,

have
mercy
on
me."

Forgiveness Word Search

DEBT   PATIENT   SEVEN
DENARII   PAY   SIN
HEART   PITY   SOLD
MERCY   SERVANT   TALENT

N D E V E R S O L D
M E R C Y S E T O P
H B F T N A V R E S
E T I O R G E S I N
A P A T I E N T I V
R A I D E N A R I I
T Y N T N E L A T G

Matthew 18:21-35
The Unforgiving Servant

Lesson 5: God is Equally Gracious to All

Activities

Cooking Activity: **Frozen Grapes**
Review Activity: **Rewards for Workers**
Group Activity: ***The Laborers in the Vineyard* Play**
Memory Work: **Review the Books of the New Testament, Part II**
Coloring Page: **Harvesters in the Vineyard**

Cooking Activity
. . . .
Frozen Grapes

In the parable, the workers were hired to work in a vineyard. Explain to the student that these grapes come from vineyards where workmen plant and trim the vines and harvest the grapes.

Materials

- Grapes, red or green, seedless
- Cookie sheet
- Waxed paper
- Available freezer space

Directions

1   Have the student help you rinse and dry the grapes (you can use a colander or salad spinner). Pick off all of the stems. While you are doing this, remind the student that Jesus' parable from this week's lesson took place in a vineyard, which is a place where grapes are grown.
2   Line the cookie sheet with the waxed paper.
3   With the student's help, arrange the grapes one by one on the waxed paper. This will allow the grapes to freeze without clumping.
4   Place the sheet of grapes in the freezer and freeze for two to three hours. Once they are frozen, they make a refreshing snack on a hot day. Remind the student that, just like the laborers in the story, someone in a real vineyard worked hard to pick these grapes.

Rewards for Workers

Materials

- Ice Cream Cones, from Student Page 45
- Digging a Ditch pictures, from Student Page 47
- Markers, crayons, or colored pencils
- Old magazines
- Child's scissors
- Glue
- FOR THE ADULT TO READ, ONLY: one secret material is needed. Look for the asterisk after the Directions to find it listed.

Directions

1   Instruct the student to color the Ice Cream Cones and the Digging a Ditch pictures from Activity pages 45 and 47. She may then cut them out, and match each Digging picture with a cone. Then help the student to glue these back to back. You should now have five ice cream cones, with varying degrees of ditch-digging labor portrayed on the backs.

2   Have the student look through old magazines, picking out four different smiling faces, each approximately one inch in diameter. Instruct the student to cut out the four faces, and to glue them onto four of the Ice Cream Cone pictures. Meanwhile, the teacher or parent should glue the secret material (see * below after Step 5) onto the fifth Cone picture, unbeknownst to the student.

3   Lay the cards out in a row, with the Ditch Digging pictures facing up. Include the fifth one at the end of the row, being sure to not let the student see the Ice Cream side.

4   Tell this story: "There was once a landowner who needed help digging a long ditch around his field. He went out to hire workers to help him. He found one willing person, and asked him or her to work on digging the ditch all day, in exchange for a gigantic, triple-scoop ice cream cone. This worker was thrilled at the idea and agreed to work! (Turn over the first card, to show the happy face of the worker, and the ice cream cone.) Halfway through the morning, the landowner went out and found another worker, who was also very excited to dig the ditch and enjoy a triple-scoop ice cream cone at the end of the day. (Turn over the second card.) At lunchtime, the landowner found a third worker, and promised him or her the same thing: a gigantic, triple-scoop ice cream cone, in exchange for working hard for the second half of the day. (Turn over the third card.) Halfway through the afternoon, the landowner found a fourth worker to help out, and promised him the same reward! (Turn over the fourth card.) That doesn't seem quite fair, does it? Well, it gets crazier: at the very end of the day, with the ditch nearly finished, the landowner went out and found one more worker, promising him or her the very same payment of a gigantic, triple-scoop ice cream cone at the end of the day. (Turn over the fifth card, revealing the student's face on the last ice cream cone!)"

5   Discuss with the student how God is like the generous landowner. We often identify with the worker from the very beginning of the day, resenting those workers who didn't have to do as much. But in truth, we are like the worker from the very end of the day! God loves us all the same, whether we have been working for him for a long time or a little while.

*Secret material: a photograph of the student's face (smiling), approximately one inch in diameter.

Group Activity

. . . .

The Laborers in the Vineyard Play

For this play, you need a minimum of six performers, but you can easily adapt the script to incorporate more people.

Materials

- *The Laborers in the Vineyard* Script (Student Pages 49–50), a copy for each student
- 1 quarter for each worker
- Highlighter marker
- OPTIONAL: Costumes for the characters (like bandanas for the workers, a robe for the landowner, etc.)

Cast of Characters
NARRATOR
LANDOWNER
WORKER 1
WORKER 2
WORKER 3
WORKER 4
FOREMAN

Directions

1   Assign the parts. The Narrator can be the instructor or a student who reads well. If you have more than seven students, you can have groups of students for Workers 1, 2, 3, and 4. Give each student a copy of the script.
2   Read through the script with the students. Have each student read his or her part. You may need to highlight the part of each player. The words in italics are stage directions, and should not be read aloud.
3   Practice the play. Have the workers sit on one side of the room (if you have groups of workers, have all the WORKER 1s sit together, etc.). The other side of the room will be the vineyard.
4   Once the play is ready, perform it for another class or for the students' parents.

Review the Books of the New Testament, Part II

Directions

1   Say to the student:
    "Last time, we reviewed the names of the books in the first half of the New Testament. Today let's review the books in the second half."
2   "After 'First and Second Thessalonians,' we learned four more books, the letters Paul sent to specific people. Let's say those together, twice:"
    [Say together, twice] First and Second Timothy, Titus, Philemon.
3   "The last set of books was written to different churches and people as messages by God, by different writers. They were Hebrews, James, First and Second Peter, First, Second, and Third John, Jude, Revelation. Let's say those names together, twice."
    [Together, twice] Hebrews, James, First and Second Peter, First, Second, and Third John, Jude, Revelation.
4   Say, "Good work. Now, take a deep breath, and let's try to say the names of <u>all</u> the books of the New Testament."
    [Together] Matthew, Mark, Luke, John, Acts, Romans, First and Second Corinthians, Galatians, Ephesians, Philippians, Colossians, First and Second Thessalonians, First and Second Timothy, Titus, Philemon, Hebrews, James, First and Second Peter, First, Second, and Third John, Jude, Revelation.

Coloring Page

Workers in the Vineyard

Here are the men from Jesus' parable, working in the vineyard. A vineyard is a place where people grow grapevines.

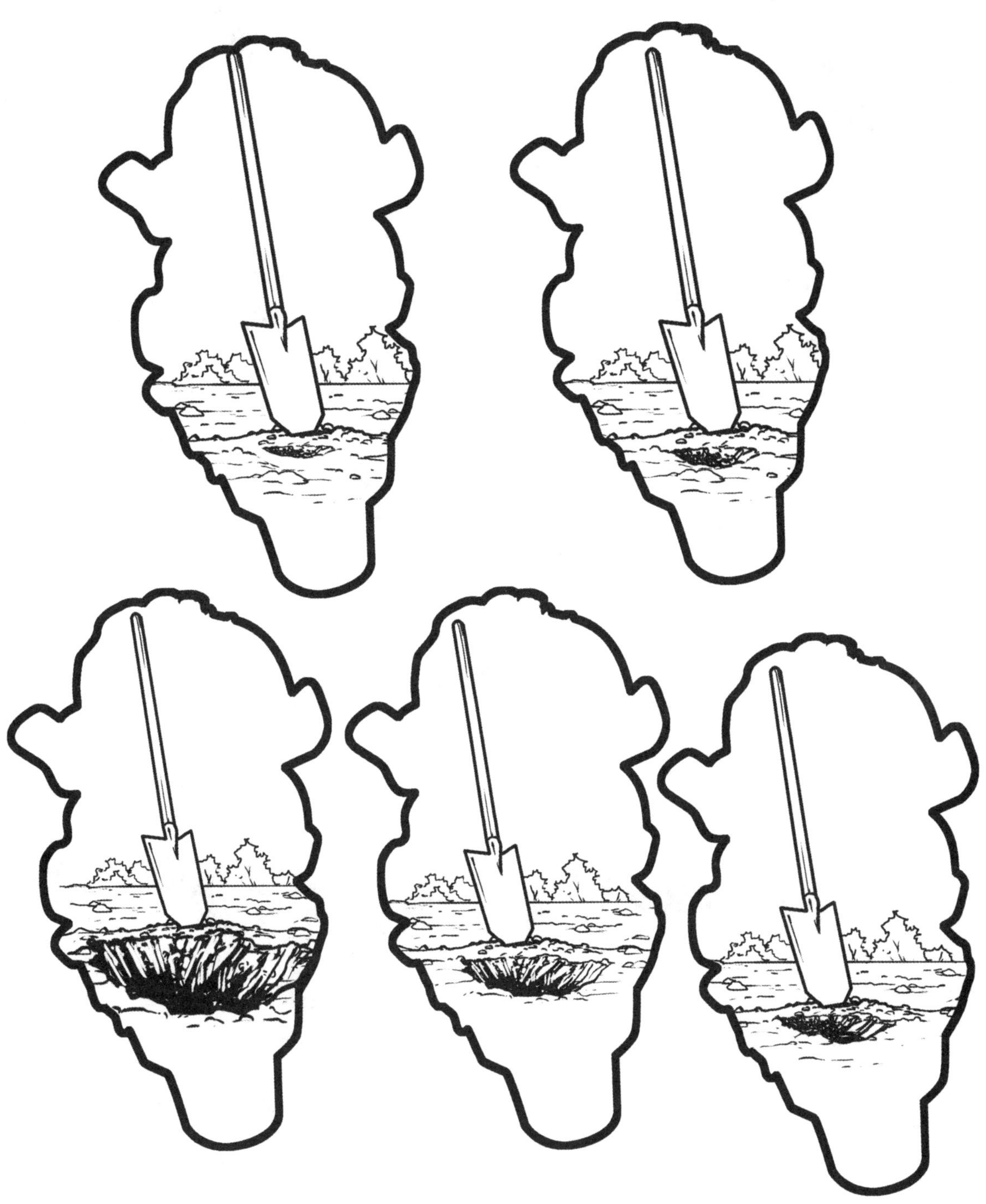

The Laborers in the Vineyard Play

NARRATOR: Once there was a landowner who needed people to work in his vineyard. He went out early in the morning and hired someone.

LANDOWNER *(says to WORKER 1):* I'll pay you a silver coin if you come and work in my vineyard all day.

WORKER 1: It's a deal!

LANDOWNER and WORKER 1 shake hands. LANDOWNER shows WORKER 1 where the vineyard is and WORKER 1 pantomimes picking grapes, clipping vines, and wiping his/her sweaty brow (it's hard work!).

NARRATOR: About midmorning the landowner goes to find another worker.

LANDOWNER *(says to WORKER 2):* If you come and work in my vineyard today, I'll pay you whatever is right.

WORKER 2: That sounds fair to me!

LANDOWNER and WORKER 2 shake hands. LANDOWNER shows WORKER 2 where the vineyard is and WORKER 2 joins WORKER 1 in the work.

WORKER 2 *(says to WORKER 1):* Wow, this is hard work. And it's hot out here!

WORKER 1: I know. I have been working out here longer than you have!

NARRATOR: After lunch the landowner goes to find another worker.

LANDOWNER *(says to WORKER 3):* Come and work in my vineyard.

WORKER 3: Okay, I'll work for you.

LANDOWNER and WORKER 3 shake hands. LANDOWNER shows WORKER 3 where the vineyard is and WORKER 3 joins WORKERS 1 and 2 in the work.

WORKER 1 *(says to WORKER 2):* Why did the landowner hire this worker?

WORKER 2 shrugs his/her shoulders.

NARRATOR: In the late afternoon, when there was only one hour left in the workday, the landowner goes to find another worker.

LANDOWNER: Why have you been sitting here all day doing nothing?

WORKER 4: Because no one hired me.

LANDOWNER: You can go work in my vineyard.

LANDOWNER and WORKER 4 shake hands. LANDOWNER shows WORKER 4 where the vineyard is. The other WORKERS look surprised to see WORKER 4. WORKER 4 joins WORKERS 1, 2, and 3 in the work.

WORKER 4 *(to other WORKERS)*: I know I probably won't get paid much for working only an hour, but I sure am happy to have this job!

NARRATOR: At the end of the day, the owner of the vineyard called his foreman.

LANDOWNER (to FOREMAN): Call all the workers and pay them their money.

FOREMAN *(points to WORKER 4)*: You there! Come and get the money you earned. *(FOREMAN hands WORKER 4 a quarter.)*

WORKER 4 *(Jumps up and down, very excited)*: Wow! I get a whole coin for just working an hour? That's amazing! That's terrific! Thank you! Thank you! *(WORKER 4 hugs the FORE-MAN and the LANDOWNER).*

FOREMAN *(points to WORKER 3)*: Here is the money you earned. *(FOREMAN hands WORKER 3 a quarter.)*

WORKER 3 *(very pleased, but not as excited as WORKER 4)*: I get a silver coin, too? That's great! Thank you very much. *(WORKER 3 shakes hand with FOREMAN and LANDOWNER.)*

FOREMAN *(points to WORKER 2)*: Here is the money you earned. *(FOREMAN hands WORKER 2 a quarter.)*

WORKER 2 *(looks a little disappointed)*: I get the same as the other two workers? Well, all right. Thank you. *(WORKER 2 nods his head at the FOREMAN and LANDOWNER.)*

WORKER 1 *(excitedly runs up to FOREMAN)*: It's my turn now! I wonder what you'll give me? I've been here the longest so I bet I'll get two or three or maybe four coins!

FOREMAN hands him a quarter.

WORKER 1: Just one coin? That's not fair! I have been here the longest! I've been working in the hot sun all day. I deserve more than the other workers!

LANDOWNER: Friend, I am not being unfair. You agreed to work for a silver coin. I want to pay the others the same as I pay you. It's my money and I have a right to do what I want with it. Take your pay and go.

NARRATOR: Jesus said the last will be first, and the first will be last. In God's kingdom, no one gets to be more important than anyone else.

Matthew 20:1–16
Workers in the Vineyard

Unit 2

Miracles Jesus Did

Lesson 6: Kings Don't Pay Taxes

Activities

Historical Craft Project: **Make a "Herod's Temple" Coin Bank and a Shekel**
Put It Into Practice Activity: **Giving Back**
Craft Project: **Make a Fish With a Coin in Its Mouth**
Group Game: **Coin, Coin, Who's Got the Coin?**
Coloring Page: **The Coin in the Fish's Mouth**

Craft/History Activity

. . . .

Make a "Herod's Temple" Coin Bank and a Shekel

Make a model of Herod's Temple (the one Jesus visited and taught in) that can be used as a coin bank. You can also make a Tyrian shekel (like the one Peter pulled from the fish's mouth), worth four drachmas, to serve as your first deposit.

Materials

- Herod's Temple Template and Tyrian Shekel Template (Student Pages 59 and 61)
- Scissors
- Pencil
- The front panel of an empty cereal box
- X-Acto knife
- Glue stick
- Clear tape (preferably clear packing tape, but Scotch tape works too)

Directions

1   Have the student cut out the Herod's Temple Template on Student Page 59. While he cuts, tell him, "This is a model of the Jewish Temple from Jesus' time, which was built by King Herod the Great. Herod the Great was appointed king of Judea by the Romans forty years before Jesus was born. He decided to rebuild the temple in Jerusalem because the old one was not in good shape. But Herod wanted this new temple to be bigger and grander than the temple had been before. What you are cutting out now is the center of the temple, the Holy of Holies, where only the priests could enter. This building was surrounded by great stone walls, columns, and courts. Work on the entire temple took a long time—over eighty years."

2   Place the Herod's Temple Template over the unmarked side of the cardboard cereal
    box. Have the student trace it with a pencil. Then have him cut the shape out of the
    cardboard.

3   Help the student use the glue stick to glue the Herod's Temple Template to the card-
    board. Do not fold it yet!

4   Using the X-Acto knife, cut the black rectangle (the coin slot) out of the cardboard
    temple.

5   Have the student fold along the dotted lines to create a box with Herod's Temple on the
    outside. Help him to secure the edges of the box with tape. Be careful not to cover the
    coin slot with tape! The side marked "Base" forms the bottom of the bank, opposite the
    surface that contains the slot.

6   To make the Tyrian shekel: have the student cut out the face and reverse of the coin
    from Student Page 61. Trace the circular outline of the coin on a piece of leftover card-
    board, cut it out, and then glue the front and back of the coin to the front and back of the
    cardboard.

7   Let the student put the shekel in the bank.

8   OPTIONAL: Combine this activity with the next activity, "Giving Back." See below.

Put It Into Practice Activity

Giving Back

If your student gets money for chores or a weekly allowance, now is a good time to introduce "giving back" some of the student's "income." Help your student understand why we do this and help him to try it out.

Directions

1   Say to the student, "Tithing is a way to give back some of the good things that God has
    given us. It is a way to show thanks to Him and to share what we have with others. In
    Bible times, people gave what grew on their farms, like grain or animals. Today, we some-
    times do it by giving money to our church, but people also give to charities, to people in
    need, or to missionaries overseas. Many people who work for the church (priests, pastors,
    missionaries) use this money to make a living."

2   Have the student try setting aside coins in the Temple Bank from the previous activity
    (either some portion from an allowance, or "found" coins, etc). Explain that the student
    is saving up these coins, instead of spending them right away, in order to give them to
    people who are in need. Try doing this for a month.

3   Help the student pick two destinations for the money: perhaps your local church or a
    local food pantry or charity.

. . . .

Make a Fish with a Coin in Its Mouth

Materials

- One 9"x12" piece of felt
- OPTIONAL: an additional small piece of felt (3"x3") in a contrasting color, for the fish's mouth
- Embroidery floss
- Felt Fish template (Student Page 63)
- Scissors
- A thick, black, permanent marker
- A couple of straight pins or safety pins
- Felt Fish mouth template (Student Page 65)
- 1 ½ cups dry, uncooked split peas or uncooked rice
- Two buttons (for fish eyes)
- One large button (for coin)
- 2" square piece of aluminum foil
- One hair elastic (the skinny kind with a metal clamp, roughly 2" diameter)
- Funnel
- Tall drinking glass
- Tape
- Sharp needle, large enough to thread embroidery floss through

Directions

1. Have the student help you carefully cut out the Fish templates and mouth template. Help the student pin the templates to the felt. If desired, use a contrasting color of felt for the mouth. Using the marker, trace each template. Cut out the three pieces.
2. Sew the small buttons onto the fish's body where the eyes would be. It helps to lay the fish out, facing each other, to make sure that you're getting the eyes placed symmetrically.
3. Put the two felt fish together, eye to eye (right sides facing). Cut a piece of embroidery floss that is 6.5' long. Thread it through the needle, and knot the two ends together. Then stitch from the "chin" of the fish (see illustration) to the center of the tail. Be sure to start at the chin. Make your stitches roughly ¼ inch long. When you get to the center of the tail, put the fish down (don't knot or cut your thread).
4. Cut hair elastic just to the side of the metal clamp. Using the needle, make a hole in the center of the felt mouth. (Don't actually thread it through.) Wiggle the needle to enlarge the hole; make it big enough for the hair elastic to fit through. Thread the large button onto the elastic, so that the metal clamp keeps it from falling off. Next thread the felt mouth onto the elastic.
5. Take the end of the elastic that has no metal clamp, and stitch it firmly to the felt tail. Then continue to stitch the two felt fish together, until you get to the "nose" of the fish. Knot and trim the thread.

6   Turn the felt fish right-side out. Place it in the
    glass, tail-down. Grab the large button, and
    pull it out of the fish and over the edge of the
    glass. Tape it to the outside of the glass. Insert
    the funnel into the fish's body. Pour in the split
    peas.
7   Carefully stitch the felt mouth to the fish's
    body, using a whipstitch.
8   Use aluminum foil to cover the large button and
    metal clamp, making them look like a coin.
9   The finished fish should look something like the
    picture in the margin.

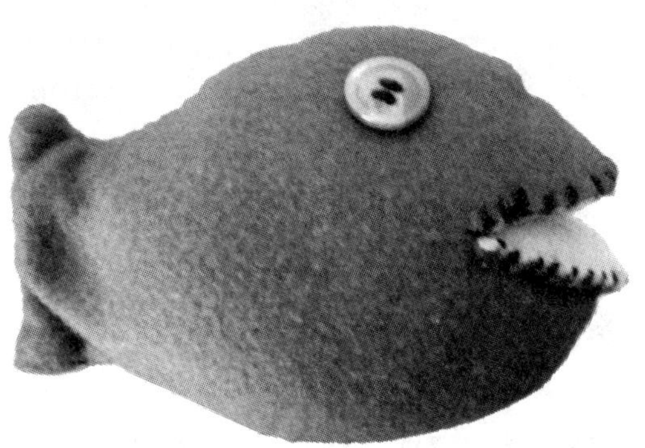

Group Game

• •

Coin, Coin, Who's Got the Coin?

This variation on "Button, Button" can be played with four or more students.

Materials

- One Coin (any coin will do, but something exotic, such as a foreign coin, will be more
  interesting)

Directions

First Option

1   Tell the students to sit in a circle, facing each other, with their hands behind their backs,
    palms cupped. Take the coin, show it to them, and say, "In this week's Bible story, Jesus
    told Peter how to find a coin in a surprising place. Now we'll have a chance to find a hid-
    den coin. I'm going to secretly drop this coin into someone's hands, but I won't show you
    whose hands I'm putting it into." Let the students know that they can pretend to receive
    the coin and that, if the coin is given to them, they can pretend that no coin fell into their
    hands!
2   Walk slowly around the outside of the circle, with your hands passing near each child's
    outstretched hands. Drop the coin into one student's hands.
3   When you have walked all the way around the circle, show that you no longer have the
    coin in your hand. Say, "Now, who's got the coin? Each of you gets one guess! Take turns
    pointing to the person who you think has the coin."
4   Have a coinless child begin the guessing as you help the students begin chanting, "Coin,
    Coin, who's got the coin?" before each guess.
5   Each student gets one guess. When a student is accused of having the coin, he should
    display his hands to show that they have no coin in them. The student who actually does
    have the coin may pretend not to, in order to point at someone else.
6   When the coin is revealed, have that student do his best fish imitation.
7   The student who guesses correctly who had the coin, becomes the next coin-distributor.
    You as the teacher may join the circle as a coin-receiver. If no one guesses who had

the coin, ask the student who has the coin to hold it up and show the group. He then becomes the next coin-distributor.

8   Ask, "If it is difficult for us to know who has the coin in our little group, and we know *somebody* has it, how did Jesus know that the fish Peter caught would have a coin in its mouth?"

Coloring Page

The Coin in the Fish's Mouth

Peter caught a fish and found a coin in its mouth, just as Jesus said would happen. (The fish in this picture is a tilapia, which may have been the kind of fish Peter caught. Fishermen still catch Tilapia in Israel today. The coin is a Tyrian shekel, which was used to pay the Temple tax.)

Herod's Temple Template

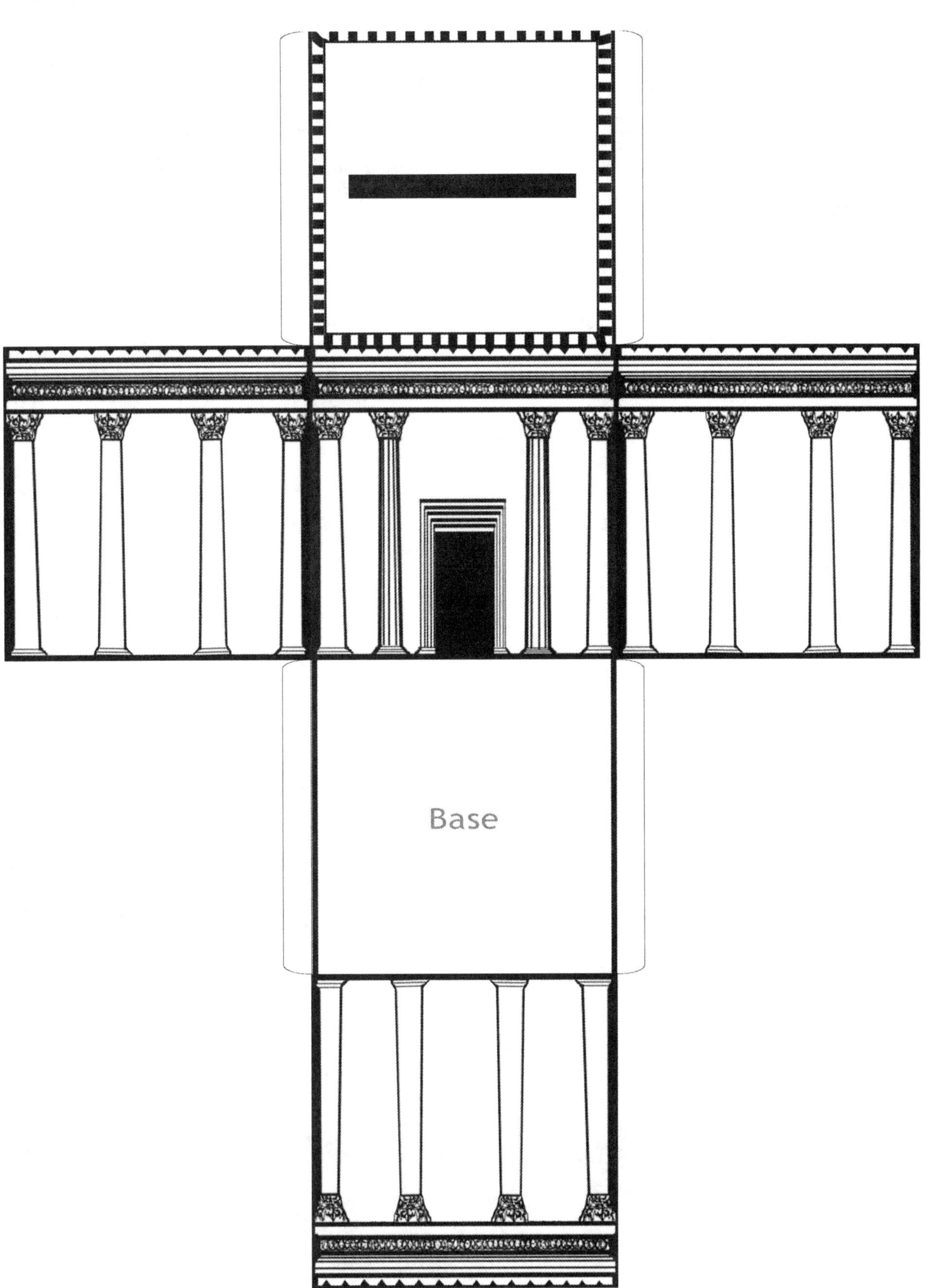

Tyrian Shekel Template

Felt Fish Template

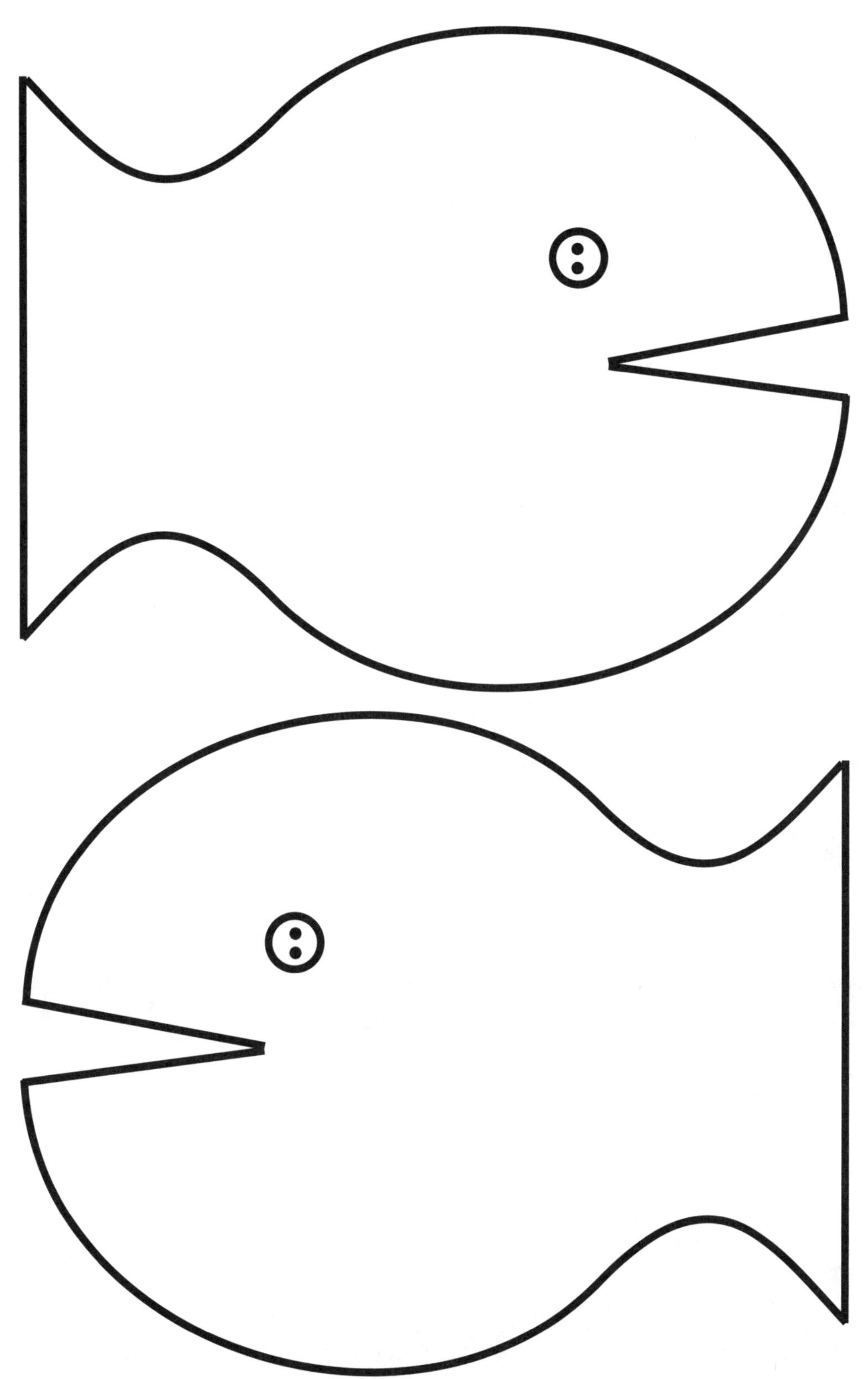

Felt Fish Mouth Template

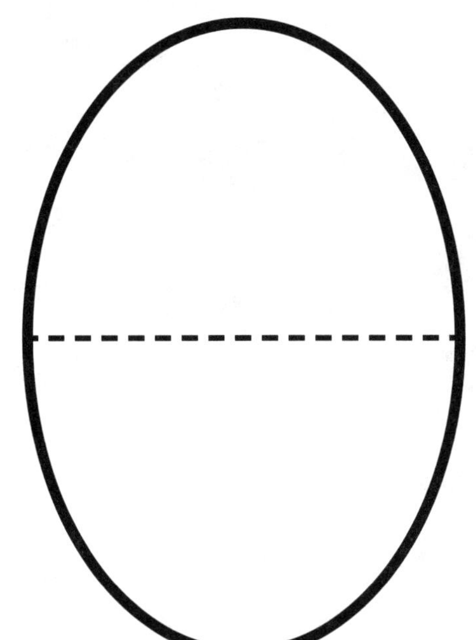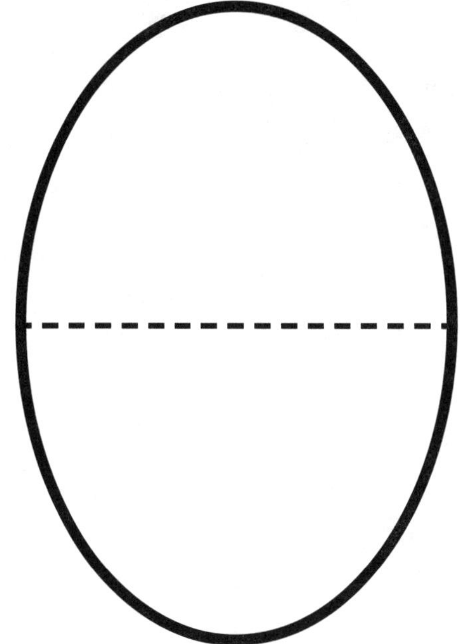

Matthew 17:24–27
The Coin in the Fish's Mouth

Lesson 7: Taking Jesus at His Word

Activities

Review Activity: **Crossword Puzzle of Jesus' Miracles**
Group Game: **Trust Game**
Coloring Page: **A Man's Faith in Jesus**

Review Activity

• •

Crossword Puzzle of Jesus' Miracles

Materials

- Pencil
- The Miracles of Jesus Crossword Puzzle (Student Page 71)

Directions

1. Have the student use the pencil to fill in the boxes of the crossword puzzle. Only one letter can go in each box. If this is the student's first experience with a crossword puzzle, explain that where two words "cross" each other, the letter where they overlap fits into both words. Give any necessary help.
2. Here is the answer key.

Answer Key

· ·

Trust Game

Materials

- Blindfold (an 18–inch strip of cloth will work)

Directions

1 Say to the student, "In today's lesson, Jesus said he would heal the man's sick son, even though the son wasn't right there with them. The man had to trust that Jesus would do what he said he would do. Today we're going to play a game where you have to trust me, because you won't be able to see what's going on."
2 Blindfold the student, making sure she can't see under, through, or over the blindfold.
3 Using verbal directions, guide the student through the house, or around your yard. ("Take one small step forward. Now put your hand straight out and you'll touch the doorknob.") Be as specific as possible to enable the student to maneuver. Stay very close, so that you will be able to catch or stop the student if she is about to run into something dangerous.

Coloring Page

· ·

A Man's Son is Healed

This man trusted that Jesus could heal his son, even from far away. When he came home from talking to Jesus, the servants told him that his son was already healed.

The Miracles of Jesus Crossword Puzzle

Across

1. Jesus restored sight to the __________ man who had faith.

2. Jesus healed the royal officer's son who was in the town of __________ while he was in Cana.

3. Jesus was asked by 10 __________ to heal them all and he did.

Down

4. Jesus instructed Peter get the __________ for the church tax out of a fish.

5. The sick woman was healed by touching Jesus' __________.

6. Jesus' first miracle was turning __________ into wine.

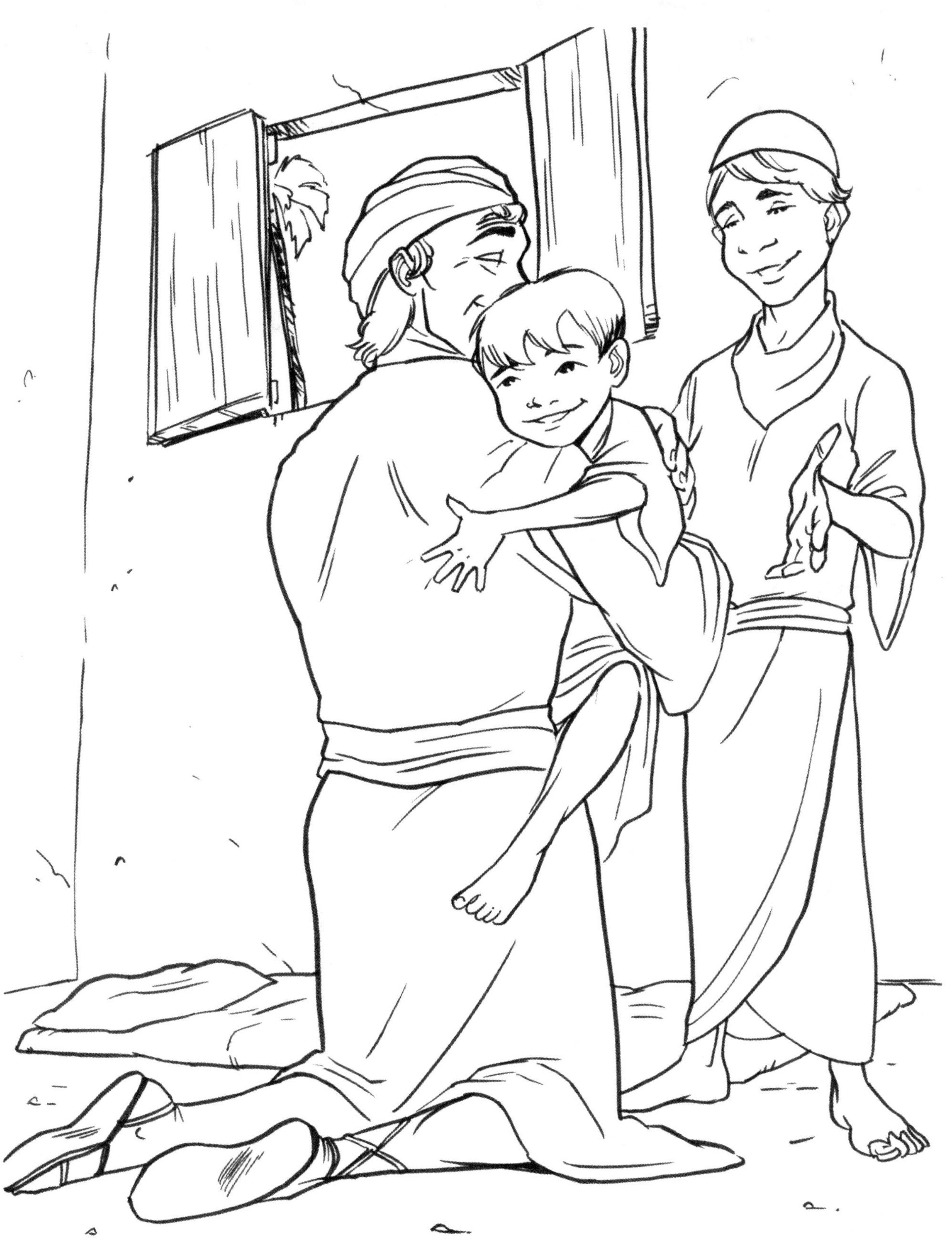

John 4:46–54
A Man's Son is Healed

Lesson 8: King Jesus Has Mercy on the Helpless

Activities

Put It Into Practice Activity: **Helping the Needy**
Put It Into Practice Activity: **Remembering to Be Thankful**
Coloring Page: **A Blind Man Calls for Help**

Put It Into Practice Activity

Helping the Needy

Directions

1 Say to the student, "In Jesus' time, needy people relied on begging and only survived on the mercy of strangers. Jesus was one who took time to help these people. Today you may or may not live in a place that has homeless or needy people begging on the sidewalk. But people in need live in every type of area. Today we're going to think of some ways that we could help people."

2 Help the student think of a way that he could help modern day "beggars" and people in dire need. Some examples:

- As a family, volunteer to serve food at a homeless shelter
- Go and read to someone in hospice care or a nursing home, or make something decorative which they can use to make their room more cheerful, or play a piece of music for them on an instrument
- On your next grocery-store trip, let the student help you pick out some food to buy and donate to a local food pantry
- If the student has an allowance, have the student save money to buy a grocery gift card and give it to a needy person
- Gather up supplies to donate to a women's shelter (these shelters usually have a website with a list of needed supplies)

3 As you plan and carry out your service, you may want to pray something like the following prayer with the student: "God, thank you for the family and food and home you have given to us. Thank you for Jesus who was kind to everyone who needed help. Please help us to be kind to people, like Jesus was."

Remembering to Be Thankful

Materials

- Jar
- Piece of paper, cut to the size of the jar
- Markers, stickers, glitter if desired
- Tape or glue
- Small strips of paper
- Pen

Directions

1 Say to the student, "In the story, after Jesus heals the man, he is so happy he follows Jesus around, praising and thanking God because he can see. Everyone else starts praising God, too. Let's think of ways you praise God each day."
2 Help the student decorate the piece of paper and to write a title across it: "Praising God" or "Thanking God." Tape or glue the paper to the jar.
3 Place the jar somewhere prominent in your home and place the strips of paper and the pen nearby.
4 Instruct everybody in the family to write down, throughout the week, ways they praised God, or things they are thankful to God for. [Examples: something fun that the family got to do that day; a place to live and play; food; a comfortable bed; a favorite toy; pleasant weather to play in; new things to learn about.] Remind the student as necessary, but don't "force" gratitude.
5 At the end of the week read all the strips of paper together as a family. Talk about whether the activity helped you remember to praise God more throughout the week.

Coloring Page

A Blind Man Calls for Help

This man called out to get Jesus' attention, and to ask Jesus to heal him, even though people around him tried to make him be quiet.

Luke 18:35–43
A Blind Man Calls for Help

Lesson 9: The Faith of the Outsiders

Activities

Review Activity: **Learn a Finger-Play and Poem**
Group Game: **Outsider Tag**
Coloring Page: **I'm Healed!**

Review Activity

Learn a Finger-Play and Poem

Learn a poem, with hand-motions, to remember the story of one man's thankfulness to Jesus.

Directions

1   Read the poem and hand-motion-directions [see below] to yourself, first, to make sure you understand them.
2   Tell the student, "Today we're going to learn a poem, with hand motions, about the Bible story from this week's lesson. Remember that in this story, Jesus healed ten people, but only one of them came back to thank him."
3   Teach the poem and the motions to the student at the same time (the motions help remind the student of the action of the poem). Take it one line at a time. The poem and motions may be too long for some students to memorize in one session; if so, spread the memorization out over a couple of days. Remember, this is supposed to be enjoyable, so do not demand precision or push the student to memorize too quickly.
4   Once the poem is learned, practice it with the student each day for the rest of the week.

Poem and directions for hand motions:

Ten lepers want to be healed,
(hold up all ten fingers)
So off they go across the field,
(hold one hand flat, palm up, and use the other hand to make a "two legs walking" motion on it)
Looking for Jesus.
(mime a "looking through binoculars" action)

Where might He be?
(hold up both hands in a shrugging, "I don't know where he is!" motion)
Seeking and searching 'til . . . what do they see?
(again, mime a "looking through binoculars" action)
It's Jesus! It's Jesus!
(clap once, excitedly, on each repetition of "Jesus")
Hip-hip hooray!
(throw your arms in the air, twice, in a celebration!)
They know he will heal them.
(use both hands to mime a "washing clean" motion across your arms and torso)
But what does he say?
(fold your arms across your chest as if you're about to give instructions)
"Go see the priest," he says to the men.
(make pointing motions toward the distance in front of you)
So off they go: 8, 9, 10.
(as you say "8, 9, 10," hold up 8 fingers, then 9, then 10, in rhythm).
And then a miracle! They were healed on their way.
(Throw up your hands in surprise!)
Healthy and well. What a marvelous day!
(Twirl all the way around to show that you are completely well!)
But one of the lepers stops in his track,
(hold up one finger) (hold one hand palm out in a "Stop!" motion)
Turns around,
(hold up one finger and turn it around)
And thinks to come back.
(hold the finger to your temple to show "thinking")
"Thank you, Jesus,
(Put your hand to your lips and arc it out and down, the sign language for "thank you")
with all of my soul,
(Hold your hands over your heart)
For healing me and making me whole."

Group Game

Outsider Tag

Materials

- A small scrap of paper for each student. All the pieces except one should have a red dot. The remaining piece should have a green dot.
- Materials for writing (blank paper, pencils or markers)

Directions

1 Tell the students, "Remember that in this week's lesson, some people had a disease that made them outcasts. They couldn't come near anyone else. But Jesus healed them."

2 Pass out the small scraps of paper to the students. Tell them to look at the dot on their piece of paper without showing it to anyone else. If they receive a red dot, they are a sick person. If they receive a green dot, they are the healer.

3 Have the healer stand in the center of the playing area and count to twenty, while all the other students back away from her. Tell everyone that when the healer has finished counting to twenty, all the other students should begin running away from her, while shouting "Unclean, unclean!" and holding one hand over their faces. The healer should try to tag the sick people.

4 If the healer tags a sick person, the sick person must run over to the writing supplies, pick up a writing instrument and a piece of paper, and write "Thank you!" three times on the paper before running and showing it to the teacher.

5 The last sick person to be tagged is the winner. He becomes the healer for the next round of the game.

Coloring Page

I'm Healed!

Ten men who had a skin disease asked Jesus to heal them. When the men realized they had been healed, only one of them came back to thank Jesus.

Luke 17:11–19
A Healed Leper Thanks Jesus

Lesson 10: Jesus Actually Touches a Dead Girl and a Sick Woman

Activities

Map Activity: **Important Places in the Life of Jesus**
Craft Project: **Cornhusk Doll**
Coloring Page: **A Woman Has Faith**

Map Activity

Important Places in the Life of Jesus

Complete this map activity to get a better sense of the places Jesus is traveling to and talking about.

Materials

- Map Key Match-Up (Student Page 89)
- Map of Important Places in the Life of Jesus (Student Page 91)
- Bible
- Pencil
- Colored pencils or fine-tip markers (blue, red, and green)

Directions

1   Tear out the Map Key Match-Up on Student Page 89. Have the student use his pencil to match the city or region with its correct description. If the student needs a hint (he probably will) then read the Bible verse provided, as a hint. *Answer Key: 1. Jerusalem, 2. Capernaum, 3. Bethlehem, 4. Jericho, 5. Nazareth, 6. GALILEE, 7. JUDEA, 8. SAMARIA*

2   Once the Map Key Match-Up is completed, go to the Map of Important Places in the Life of Jesus (Student Page 91). First, have the student use the blue pencil to trace the edge of the Mediterranean Sea, the path of the Jordan River, and the perimeter of the Sea of Galilee and the Dead Sea.

3   Each town or city on the map is marked with the numbers 1–5. Using the Map Key Match-Up, write the name of each city in red next to its corresponding number on the map. *Answer Key: 1. Jerusalem, 2. Capernaum, 3. Bethlehem, 4. Jericho, 5. Nazareth*

4   Each region on the map is marked with the numbers 6–8. Using the Map Key Match-Up,
     write the name of each region in ALL CAPITALS next to its corresponding number on
     the map. *Answer Key: 6. GALILEE, 7. JUDEA, 8. SAMARIA*

Craft Project

Corn Husk doll with cloak

*In this week's story, Jesus returned a little girl to life, allowing her to be healthy and to play again.
Corn was not grown in first-century Palestine, so the girl didn't have a corn husk doll, but simple
dolls much like this one have been played with by children around the world for millennia.*

Materials

- Large mixing bowl of cold water
- Some kind of waterproof weight (a rock will work)
- 15 corn husks (used for wrapping tamales; can be found in the pro-
  duce department of a grocery store) **See Figure 1**
- Small towel
- String
- Piece of cloth the size of a bandana (knit is best, so it does not
  unravel)
- Scissors

FIGURE 1

Directions

*Throughout this project tie all your knots at the BACK of the doll
so they are not as visible.*

1   Take out two bunches of husks (about ten)
     from the bag and soak them in cold water
     for several hours; overnight is all right too.
     Put a weight down on them so they do not
     float back up to the top and so that they are
     completely submerged. **Figure 2**
2   After they have soaked, take them out and
     peel them apart and lay them on a towel to
     drain, but do not let them dry. **Figure 3**
3   Choose four corn husks that are about the
     same size and that are not torn. Lay one
     down; then put two on top of it, side by
     side, and the fourth one on top of the first.
     Figure 4
4   Tie towards the top of the flat edges of
     the corn husk (so that the top edges are
     bunched together). Trim the ends of the tied
     string. **Figure 5**

FIGURE 2

FIGURE 3

FIGURE 4

FIGURE 5

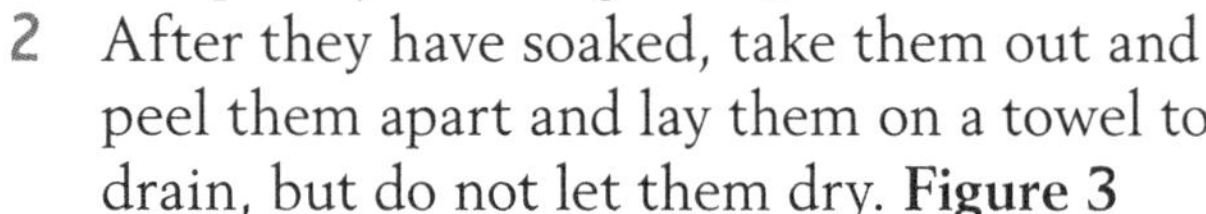

5   [The instructor should supervise this step]
    Trim off some extra husk above the string.
    Turn it upside down and gently pull the
    husks down over the short end that has been
    tied and trimmed. **Figure 6**

6   Gather the husks over the stub end to form
    the head and tie off below the stub (what
    will be the neck), that is now instead the
    doll's head. Trim the ends of the string.
    Figure 7

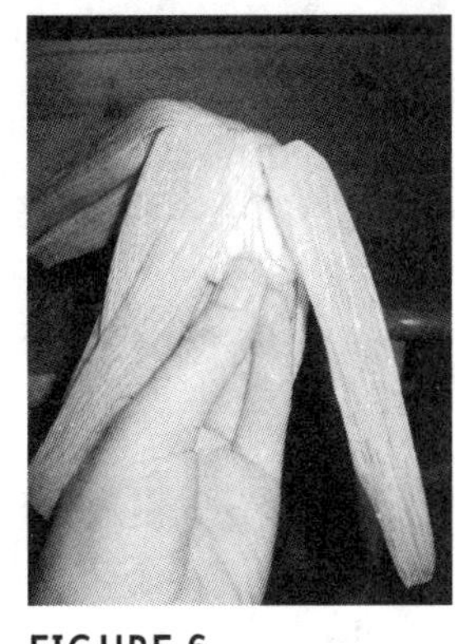

FIGURE 6

FIGURE 7

7   Take a single husk and roll it up
    the long way. This will be the "arms." Tie off
    at each end, around the "wrists" about ⅓ of an
    inch from the end. Trim the string ends. You may trim the arms to
    shorten them, or use your scissors to shape some hands.

8   Below the tie where the loose bunch of
    husks is now hanging down, separate the
    loose pieces into two bunches. Then slide
    the long piece you made in step 7 between
    those two bunches as high up as it will go,
    so that it is just below the tie for the head
    that you made in step 6. Now your doll
    has two "arms." Below the arms, tie the two
    bunches together again around the waist to
    secure the arms in place. Trim string. **Figure
    8**

FIGURE 8

FIGURE 9

9   Take two additional husks and fold them
    vertically. Place them on a surface in an X
    shape with the skinnier ends at the top. Lay
    the doll in the middle of the X. **Figure 9**

10 Bring the narrow ends down diagonally over
    the doll's shoulders. Do not tie or secure
    these yet, just hold them in place with one
    hand. **Figure 10**

11 With your other hand, take two more husks
    and lay them at waist level on the doll's left

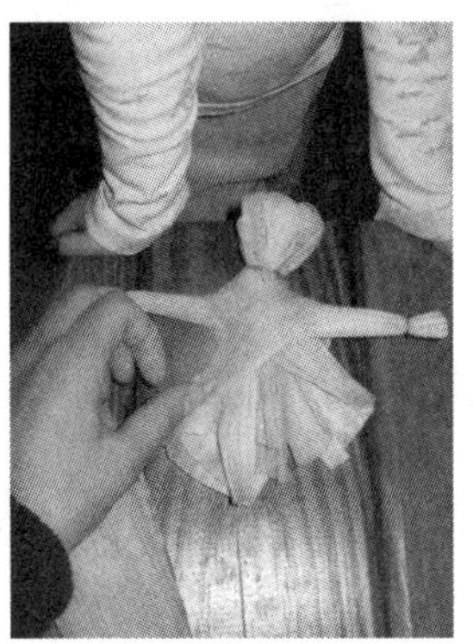

FIGURE 10

FIGURE 11

    side, with the narrow part hanging down. Do the same on the doll's
    right side. Tie a piece of string around the doll's midsection in such
    a way that it ties these husks on, while it secures the pieces that are
    now forming an X-shape across the doll's chest. Trim string. **Figure
    11**

12 Divide the corn husks hanging from the bottom on two sides for
    two legs. Split some of the husks up the middle to divide them
    evenly if needed. Tie around each thigh and trim string. Do the
    same at the knees and the ankles. Trim the feet at the desired
    length and the desired shape. **Figure 12**

FIGURE 12

Sew-less Cloak

1. Fold the bandanna-sized piece of cloth in half, vertically, and lay your doll on it, with the doll's neck resting on the fold. Have the doll's arm at one end of the fabric and cut the fabric up at the end of the doll's other hand.
2. Remove the doll and cut a small neck hole in the middle.
3. Cut a slit up the front of the cloak for an opening. When you open it up it should look like **Figure 13.**
4. Fold the cloth back in half and drape over the doll with opening in front. Cut out some of the straight fabric under the arms to give it a curved cloak shape on either side. **Figure 14**
5. Wrap the back part of the cloak around the front of the waist, under the front cloak flaps. Bunch the sleeves into a good position as you go.
6. Wrap the front cloak flaps around the back, on top of the back cloak flaps.
7. Secure with string around the waist. **Figure 15**

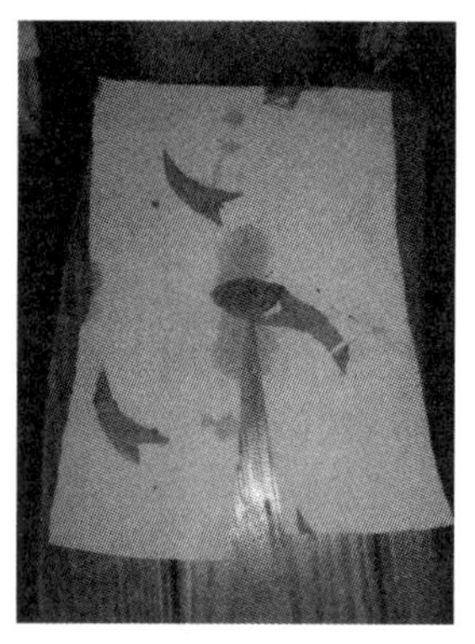

FIGURE 13

FIGURE 14

FIGURE 15

Coloring Page

A Woman Has Faith

This woman believed that Jesus could heal her. She was afraid, so she only touched his cloak, but Jesus wasn't angry with her. He was kind and he healed her.

Map Key Match-Up

1. This important city contained the Temple. This is where Jesus told the story of the two sons—the one who obeyed and the one who didn't (Lesson 1). HINT: Read John 4:20.

Capernaum

2. Jesus spent a lot of time in this city during his ministry. He often stayed in the home of his disciple Peter, who was from here. This is where the temple tax collectors asked for money (Lesson 6). HINT: Read Matthew 17:24.

SAMARIA

Bethlehem

3. This is the town where Jesus was born. HINT: It is the first city mentioned in Matthew 2:1.

4. In the story of the Good Samaritan (Lesson 3), Jesus says the injured traveler was on his way from Jerusalem to this city. HINT: Read Luke 10:30

JUDEA

5. Jesus grew up in this town. HINT: Read Luke 4:16.

Nazareth

6. This region is near the Sea of Galilee. Many people who lived here farmed or fished. Jews had lived in this area since ancient times. HINT: Read Matthew 28:10.

GALILEE

7. This region stretches from the coast to the Salt Sea. Many Jews live here, as it contains the city of Jerusalem.

Jerusalem

8. This region lies directly between Galilee and Judea, although traveling Jews would avoid walking through here because they did not like the people who lived here. HINT: Read John 4: 4.

Jericho

Important Places in the Life of Jesus

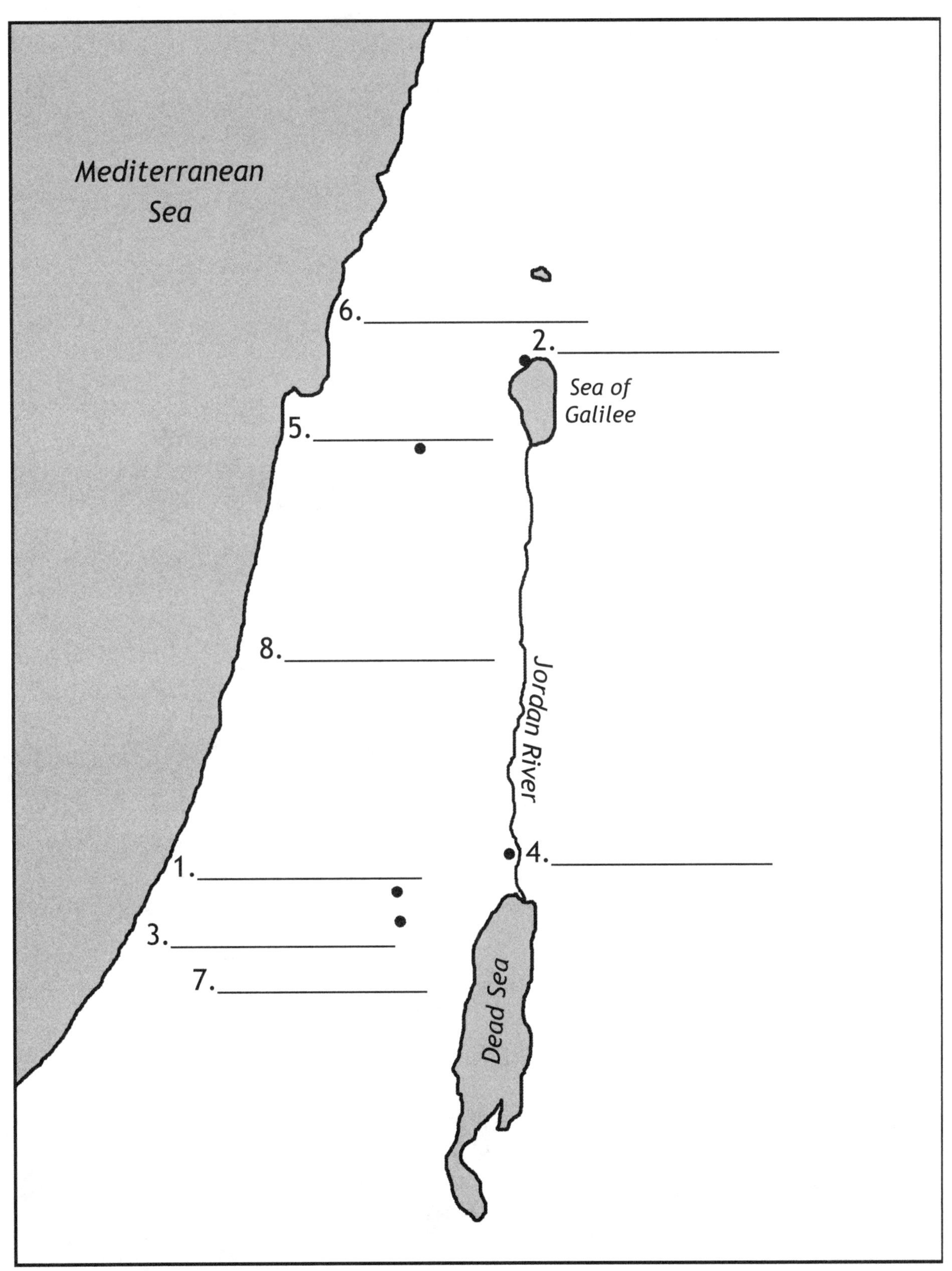

Matthew 9:18–26
A Woman Has Faith

Unit 3
Teachings of Jesus

Lesson 11: God Loves the Rich and the Poor the Same

Activities

Group Game: **Musical Chairs With a Twist**
Activity: **Dinner Party for Unloved Stuffed Animals**
Coloring Page: **Competing for the Best Seat**

Group Game

Musical Chairs With A Twist

Materials

- Chairs, one fewer than the number of players
- Music source such as a CD player, radio, or iPod
- A comfortable cushion

Directions

1 Set up the chairs in a long row.
2 Explain the basic premise of Musical Chairs to the players, if they are not already familiar with it: "While the music plays, we will all march around the row of chairs. When the music stops, run and sit in a chair as quickly as you can." Mention that the seat with the cushion is a special seat of honor, but don't specifically instruct the players to try to sit in it. Remind them that the game will have a twist at the end, one that teaches something about how Jesus loves us.
3 Play the game one time.
4 When the scuffle is over, one person will be left without a chair. Lead that person over to the seat with the cushion, and have those two people trade places. Explain how Jesus came to invite those who are left out to have a special place of honor.

<hr>

Dinner Party for Unloved Stuffed Animals

Materials

- Stuffed animals, other toys
- Food or "pretend/play food"
- Utensils

Directions

1. Have the student search her room for any stuffed animals, or any toys, that have not been played with for a long time.
2. Set a table, or a picnic blanket, with place settings. Set out the food (or play food.)
3. Have a dinner for the neglected stuffed animals, the student, and you. Have the student go around the circle while you eat and tell each one that she loves them, and what a fun time she had playing with them.

Coloring Page

<hr>

Competing for the Best Seat

These men are arguing over the best seat at the meal, the seat that is closest to the host of the party. Jesus said that we aren't supposed to fight over getting people's attention.

Luke 14:7–14
Competing for the Best Seat

Lesson 12: No One's Sins are Too Big for God to Forgive

Activities

History/Cooking Activity: **Eat an Ancient Snack on the Floor**
Group Game: **Burden Tag**
Coloring Page: **A Forgiven Sinner is Grateful**

History/Cooking Activity

· ·

Snack on the Floor

This week's Bible story took place at a meal. This activity helps your student experience a first-century Mediterranean meal time.

Materials

- Several of the following foods, whichever your student would prefer. (These are foods that could have been eaten at a Judean or Galilean meal in Jesus' time.)
    - Cheese
    - Dates
    - Figs
    - Raisins
    - Pistachios
    - Apples
    - Cucumbers
    - Melon
    - Pomegranates
    - Hard boiled eggs
    - Milk
    - Water
    - Grape juice
    - Honey
- Pita Bread (store-bought, OR make your own, using the recipe from *Telling God's Story Activity Book 1*, p. 72)
- Cucumber-Yogurt Dip (see recipe at the end of the Materials list)

  - Large cloth
  - Pillows and cushions
  - OPTIONAL: a table-sized sheet of plywood and four bricks or blocks

Cucumber-Yogurt Dip
- 1 cucumber, sliced lengthwise, seeds scooped out, peeled and finely grated
- 8 oz plain yogurt
- 3 sprigs mint, finely chopped
- Half a clove garlic, minced
- 3 Tbs lemon juice
- Salt to taste
- Medium bowl

Strain the extra liquid from the yogurt and put the yogurt in a bowl. Add remaining ingredients and mix. Use as dip for pita bread.

Directions

1. Say to the student, "In the place and time where Jesus was teaching, most people didn't sit on chairs at a table when they ate. Often they lay on cushions or rugs, around a low table. Today, we're going to eat some foods that Jesus and his disciples might have eaten, and we'll eat on the floor, like they did."
2. Prepare any combination of the above foods that would appeal to your student.
3. Spread a cloth directly on the floor as your "table," or get a large piece of plywood and prop it up on four bricks. Cover the wood with a cloth and lay pillows all around the table.
4. To get settled at the table, lie on your sides, propped on the pillows, with your feet pointing away from the table. Use one arm to support yourself on the pillows and eat with the other hand.
5. As you eat your meal, you can discuss this week's story with your student.

Group Game

Burden Tag

Materials

- Small bucket or gallon container full of water, one per student

Directions

1. One student is "it." He chases all the other students, like regular tag.
2. The instructor stands nearby, next to the containers of water.
3. When the student who is "it" tags one of the other students, the tagged student must stop and stay in one place. The instructor brings that student a bucket or gallon jug filled with water, and the student must hold that jug out in front of himself.
4. Any other student who is not "it" can tag the students who are burdened with water.

When these students are tagged, they have been "freed" and so they can put down their burden and run around again.

5   After the game is over, say to the students, "Wasn't it hard to hold up those heavy jugs of water? Weren't you relieved and happy when someone tagged you and freed you from having to hold that heavy burden? In today's lesson, we heard about how Jesus forgives people for the bad things they do. Jesus said that people who are forgiven for these sins will be relieved and grateful, not to have to feel sad anymore for what they did."

Coloring Page

A Forgiven Sinner is Grateful

This woman is wiping Jesus' feet. She is doing this because she's so grateful that he forgives her for the things she has done. Jesus said that when God forgives people they will be very grateful.

Luke 7:36–50
A Forgiven Sinner is Grateful

Lesson 13: Jesus is the Shepherd who Loves His Sheep

Activities

Group Game: **Defend the Sheep!**
Craft Project: **Shepherd's Belt**
Cooking Activity: **Good Shepherd's Pie**
Memory Work: **Psalm 23, Part I**
Coloring Page: **A Shepherd Defends His Sheep**

Group Game

Defend the Sheep!

In today's lesson, the student learned how protective a shepherd is of his sheep. This fun group game helps reinforce that concept.

Materials

- Empty paper-towel roll or empty wrapping-paper tube
- Old blanket, tarp, or sheet that can be laid on the ground

Directions (this game works best with at least 4 players, and is most fun when played outdoors)

1 Pick one student to be the Shepherd, one to be the Wolf, and the rest to be the Sheep. If you are playing with a very large group, you can assign multiple students to be Wolves. The Shepherd's goal is to keep the Sheep from being tagged. The Wolf's goal is to tag as many sheep as possible.

2 Use the blanket, tarp, or sheet to designate a space to be the "sheepfold," the place where the Sheep are trying to spend the night. Have the Sheep go into the "sheepfold" space and crouch on hands and knees, or sit down. Tell them that they can make sheep noises if they want to, but they must not speak. The sheep should stay inside the boundaries of the sheepfold unless tagged by the Wolf (see Step 5).

3 Select an area or object, twenty feet from the sheepfold. This is the Wolf's "den."

4 Tell the Shepherd that she must protect the Sheep with her "staff" (the paper towel roll). But she must not go more than five feet from the edge of the sheepfold (show her how far this is).

5   The Wolf starts at his den and tries to run to the sheepfold and tag as many Sheep as possible. The Wolf can tag sheep by going inside the sheepfold or reach into the sheepfold from the outside. Every Sheep that he tags has to walk out of the sheepfold area and over to the "wolf den." But if the Shepherd touches the Wolf with his "staff," the Wolf has to stop immediately and return to the den, before trying again.

6   The game ends when either: a) all the sheep are tagged or b) the Wolf has been tagged 3 times by the Shepherd. If you'd like to play another round, pick a new Shepherd and Wolf and begin again.

Craft Project

Shepherd's Belt

Materials

- Yarn, in 5 different colors
- Scissors
- Clamp or clothespin to hold the strands steady

Directions

1   Take a ball of yarn in one of the colors, and string it around the student's waist, twice. This tells you the length of yarn you will need. Using the scissors, cut that amount of yarn off the ball (note that it's always better to start with too long a piece—you can always cut some off at the end of the project).

2   Using that first piece as a guide, cut two strands of each color of yarn to that same length. You should end with ten strands, two of each color, all of equal length.

3   When you have all the strands cut, hold all the strands together at one end, letting the strands hang down from your hand. Look at them to make sure they are not tangled, and have no knots.

4   With the end that you have in your hand, make a knot. (Do this by wrapping the yarn around your first two fingers to make a loop. Then pull all the ends, together, tightly through that loop.)

5   Use the clip or clamp to secure the knotted end of the yarn to a surface, so that you can have both hands free. (You might try securing it to the bottom hem of the shirt you're wearing, or to the knee of your trousers.) Now pull all the strands firmly so they stick straight out.

6   See Diagram 1, to the right. Use this diagram to arrange the yarn into the correct starting pattern. Assign a number to each color of yarn you are using, and then arrange the strands to match the numbers on the diagram. (For instance, if you gave your red yarn the number "1," there should be one red strand on the Top Right side, and one on the Top Left side . . . and so on.)

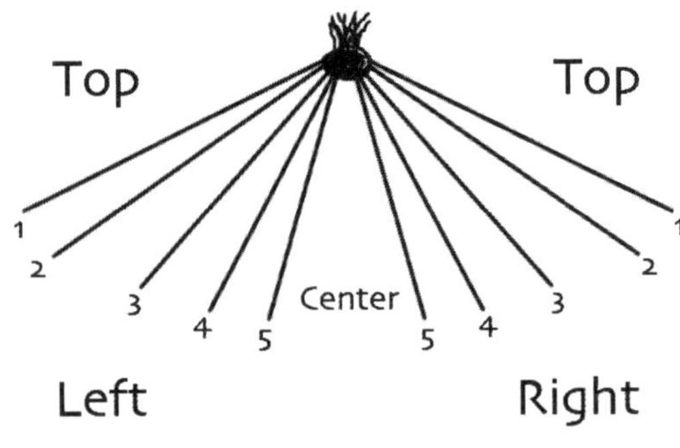

DIAGRAM 1

7   Once your strands are arranged as in Diagram
    1, take Strand 1 on the Top Left side, and place
    it between Strand 5 on the Right, and the
    center line, crossing over the top of the four
    strands on the left, and the center. See Diagram
    2 for help.

8   Take Strand 1 on the Top Right side, and place
    it in the center-left, crossing over all five of the
    strands on the right.

9   Take Strand 2 on the Top Left side, and place
    it in the center-right, crossing over the four
    strands on the left.

10 Take Strand 2 on the Top Right side, and place it in the center-left, crossing over the five
    strands on the right.

11 Continue this pattern with all five Left strands and all five Right strands (you will
    start to see a V-shaped pattern) until you have a hand span (5 to 6 inches) of free yarn
    remaining.

12 Pinch the belt at the end of the braided section. While pinching the free ends of the
    strands in one hand, unfasten the clip or clamp from the other end of the pattern.

13 While still holding the free ends together, wrap the entire belt around the student's waist
    to check for fit. Leave a couple of extra inches for the belt-fastening knot. (It it seems too
    long, use scissors to cut it to a better length, then unravel an inch or two for knot-tying.)

14 If it seems to be the correct size, knot the unfinished end with a slip knot. [If you haven't
    done a slip knot before, here are the steps: pinch the unfinished end into a loop with your
    left hand. Fold the loop down against the front of the
    belt. The loose ends should lie against the braid (See
    Diagram 3). Stick your right index finger through the
    right side of the loop and then, with your right index
    finger and thumb, grab the left side of the loop and pull
    it back through the right side.]

15 Now that the belt has knots at both ends, wrap it
    around the child's waist, so that the slip knot end is on
    the left and the other knot is on the right. Feed the right
    knot through the loop of the slip knot, and gently tug
    it until the belt tightens to the desired length. Grab the
    left side of the belt and pull until tight. (Optional: cut
    off any trailing strands that remain.)

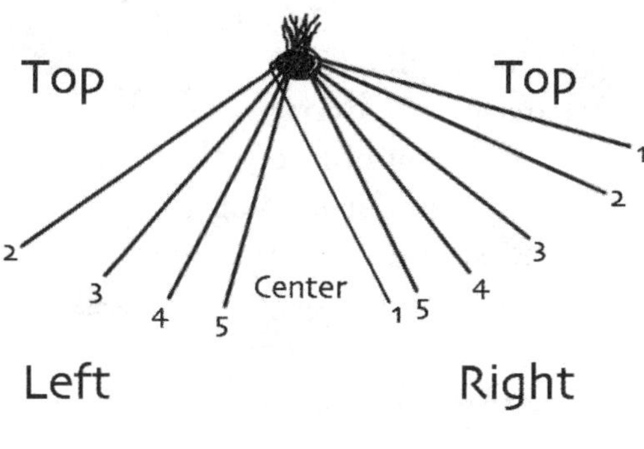

DIAGRAM 2

DIAGRAM 3

Cooking Activity

Good Shepherd's Pie (Vegetarian)

Ingredients

- 1 cup lentils, green or French, rinsed
- 2 lbs potatoes or sweet potato (We used 3 large potatoes and 1 sweet potato)

- 2 Tablespoons butter
- ¼ cup milk
- 1 teaspoon olive oil
- 1 small onion, finely chopped
- ½ teaspoon ground cumin
- ½ teaspoon dried thyme
- 1 teaspooon apple cider vinegar
- 1 Tablespoon ketchup
- 5 drops Tabasco sauce
- 1 cup frozen sweet corn
- Salt and pepper

Directions

1   Place lentils in a medium pot and cover with an inch of cold water. Add a pinch of salt, cover and bring to a boil. Reduce heat to medium low and simmer for 20 minutes until cooked. It is okay if they are not completely cooked, they will cook further later. Drain.
2   While lentils are cooking, peel and roughly chop potatoes. Place in a pot and cover with cold water. Add a teaspoon of salt to the water and bring to a boil. Simmer until potatoes are tender.
3   Drain potatoes and mash. Add butter and milk and season with salt and pepper. Cover and set aside.
4   Heat oil in a medium pot and add chopped onion. Sautée for a few minutes until soft. Add cumin, thyme, cooked lentils, vinegar, ketchup, Tabasco sauce, ½ teaspoon salt and pepper to taste. Stir to combine.
5   Add ½ cup of water and bring lentils to a simmer. Cook for another five minutes or so, stirring often, to let the flavors come together.
6   Preheat oven to 375°F. Place seasoned lentils in the bottom of a medium baking dish. Spread to cover the bottom. Top with corn kernels. Add mashed potatoes on top and spread evenly. Bake for about 30 minutes until heated through. Serve hot.

Memory Work

Psalm 23, Part I

Note to Instructor: In this activity, the student will begin to memorize Psalm 23, which she'll finish learning in Lessons 14 and 15. The modern-language New International Version may be easier to understand, but the language of the older King James Version is famous and may be familiar to the child from church or home. We have provided the wording from both versions; choose the one that will be easiest for your child to remember.

Materials

- Psalm 23, Part I (Student Page 113 or 115, depending on which version you choose)

Directions

1 Tear out Psalm 23, Part I on Student Page 113 or 115, depending on which version you'd like the student to memorize.

2 Say to the student:
"In this week's lesson, we learned that Jesus takes care of us, like a shepherd takes care of sheep. There is a very famous poem from the Bible that talks about this, and we are going to start memorizing it today. It talks about God being our shepherd, who protects us (with a staff like shepherds used) and gives us what we need, so that we don't lack. First, I will read it to you."

3 Read aloud to the student, either the King James or New International Version:

KJV
The Lord is my shepherd; I shall not want.
He maketh me to lie down in green pastures;
He leadeth me beside the still waters;
He restoreth my soul.
He leadeth me in paths of righteousness for his name's sake.
Yea, though I walk through the valley of the shadow of death,
I will fear no evil, for thou art with me.
Thy rod and thy staff, they comfort me.
Thou preparest a table before me, in the presence of mine enemies.
Thou anointest my head with oil;
My cup overflows.
Surely goodness and mercy will follow me all the days of my life,
And I will dwell in the house of the Lord forever.

NIV
The Lord is my shepherd, I shall not be in want.
He makes me lie down in green pastures,
He leads me beside quiet waters, he restores my soul.
He guides me in paths of righteousness for his name's sake.
Even though I walk through the valley of the shadow of death,
I will fear no evil, for you are with me. Your rod and your staff, they comfort me.
You prepare a table before me in the presence of my enemies. You anoint my head with oil; my cup overflows. Surely goodness and love will follow me all the days of my life,
And I will dwell in the house of the Lord forever.

4 Today, help the student learn the first third of the psalm. Begin by having her repeat the first line after you, three times. Then add the second verse. Try, today, to help her learn the psalm up to "He restores my soul." Remember to review at least once a day (twice is even better) for the next few days. Use the Student Page as a memory aid. The student may also enjoy drawing a sheep or a shepherd or some green pastures on this page.

Coloring Page

• •

A Shepherd Defends His Sheep

This shepherd is standing at the entrance to the sheepfold (the place where sheep spend the night). He loves his sheep. When wolves try to eat the sheep (like the Arabian wolves in this picture) he doesn't run away; he uses his staff to protect the flock.

Psalm 23, Part I
(King James Version)

The Lord is my shepherd; I shall not want.

He maketh me to lie down in green pastures;

He leadeth me beside the still waters;

He restoreth my soul.

Psalm 23, Part I
(New International Version)

The Lord is my shepherd, I shall not be in want.

He makes me lie down in green pastures,

He leads me beside quiet waters, he restores my soul.

John 10:11–21
A Shepherd Defends His Sheep

Lesson 14: Jesus is Greater Than Death

Activities

Craft Project: **"I Belong to Jesus" Photo Frame**
Memory Work: **Psalm 23, Part II**
Coloring Page: **Jesus and Martha**

Craft Project

. . . .

"I Belong to Jesus" Photo Frame

Materials

- Craft foam, 2 sheets
- Ribbon
- 4" x 6" photo of your student
- Puff paint (available at craft stores)
- Glue
- Scissors

Directions

1. As you're preparing the craft, say to the student, "In this week's lesson you learned that throughout your whole life, no matter where you go, you belong to Jesus."
2. Take the craft foam, and cut out a "back" for your photo frame, about 4.5" x 6.5". You can make rounded corners if you prefer.
3. Using this back as your guide, have the student cut out the front as a matching piece. Then have him cut out the middle of the front piece, leaving a one inch border between the hole and the edge.
4. Help the student glue his photo to the back of the frame.
5. Secure a piece of ribbon at the top of the frame as a loop for hanging, making it well-balanced and gluing the ribbon ends near each corner of the frame. Let the student glue the front part of the frame on top of the picture.
6. Have the student use the puff paint to write the phrase "I Belong to Jesus." Hang it for your student in his bedroom or someplace where he can see it and be encouraged by it.

Psalm 23, Part II

Materials

- Psalm 23, Part II (Student Page 121 or 123, depending on which version you choose)

Directions

1. Tear out Psalm 23, Part II, on Student Page 121 or 123, depending on your version.
2. Say to the student, "You've been learning the first part of this poem. Today you will learn some more of it."
3. Begin by helping the student recite the first ⅓ of the psalm.
   Next, teach him a new line, by having him repeat it after you or say it with you at least three times: "He guides me in paths of righteousness for his name's sake." Continue in this way until the student can say the psalm through ". . . they comfort me."
4. Where necessary, explain unfamiliar words or concepts to the student. "Valley of the shadow of death" could be "times that are scary." A shepherd's staff was a long stick used to gently guide the sheep in the right direction; a "rod" was a club that could be used to protect the sheep from wolves and other animals who might harm them.
5. Review the psalm with the student over the following days.

Coloring Page

Jesus and Martha

Martha and Mary and their friends are sad because their brother Lazarus has died. Jesus is sad too, but he is telling Martha that he is going to bring Lazarus back to life. Jesus is stronger than death.

Psalm 23, Part II
(King James Version)

The Lord is my shepherd; I shall not want.

He maketh me to lie down in green pastures;

He leadeth me beside the still waters;

He restoreth my soul.

He leadeth me in paths of righteousness for his name's sake.

Yea, though I walk through the valley of the shadow of death,

I will fear no evil, for thou art with me.

Thy rod and thy staff, they comfort me.

Psalm 23, Part II
(New International Version)

The Lord is my shepherd, I shall not be in want.

He makes me lie down in green pastures,

He leads me beside quiet waters, he restores my soul.

He guides me in paths of righteousness for his name's sake.

Even though I walk through the valley of the shadow of death,

I will fear no evil, for you are with me. Your rod and your staff,

they comfort me.

John 11:17–27
Jesus and Martha

Lesson 15: Staying Connected to Jesus

Activities

Science Activity: **Nature Hike: The Life of Trees**
Cooking Activity: **Make Your Own Grape Juice**
Group Game: **Stay Connected to the Vine**
Memory Work: **Psalm 23, Part III**
Coloring Page: **The Fruitful Vine**

Science Activity

Nature Hike—the Life of Trees

Materials

- Pencil or pen
- Student Page 131, "Nature Hike," with list of items to find on your walk
- OPTIONAL: a pocket guide to trees such as the *Fandex Family Field Guide*

Directions

1 Tear out Student Page 131, "Nature Hike," which contains a list of items to look for.
2 Take the student for a walk, looking for trees and plants in different stages of growth. Each time you or the student sees one of the items on the list, encourage the student to take a close look at it. Then have the student check off that item on the paper.
3 During or after your walk, remind the student: "In today's lesson, Jesus said that all of us who love him and try to do what he says are like branches on a tree. He says that if we stop doing what he says, and stop trusting him, we'll be like dried up old branches. But if we are with him, our lives will show people good things, just like these healthy trees and plants that we see."

• •

Make Your Own Grape Juice

Materials

- Grapes (2 pounds or more)*
- Strainer for rinsing
- Potato masher
- Large pot
- Spoon for stirring
- Second pot or similar-sized container or bowl
- Cheesecloth
- Drinking glasses
- OPTIONAL: Rubber bands

Pick grapes or buy them at the store; any kind will do but seedless ones are best. The fall is a wonderful time to pick grapes or find fresh local ones in the supermarket. A pound of grapes will make a little less than one cup of juice.

Directions

1   Have the student help you wash and de-stem the grapes. Discard un-ripened or old shriveled grapes.
2   With the student's help, mash the grapes. You can do this with your hands, or you can use a potato masher.
3   Put the grapes into a large pot. Slowly heat the grapes and then simmer on medium heat for 10 minutes, stirring occasionally and breaking them up as you go.
4   Using cheesecloth, strain the grapes with the student's help. Put cheesecloth over another pot or container (use rubber bands to secure it if you wish). Ladle out the mixture and strain through the cheesecloth. Pour the final contents of the pot onto the cheesecloth and let it sit for several hours to finish straining.
5   Remove the cheesecloth and rinse it. Sediment will have formed at the bottom of your juice; strain through the cheesecloth one more time and then chill your juice prior to drinking.

• •

Stay Connected to the Vine

Materials

- Three sheets of paper
- Marker
- Scissors
- 18–inch strip of cloth to use as a blindfold

Directions

1 Before class, cut each of the sheets of paper in half, thus creating six smaller sheets.
2 Using the marker, write this sentence across the six sheets of paper: "Jesus is the Vine; we are the branches," breaking it up into pieces, like this:

> First sheet: Jesus
> Second sheet: is
> Third sheet: the Vine
> Fourth sheet: we
> Fifth Sheet: are
> Sixth Sheet: the branches

3 You, the teacher, will act as the "Vine." The students have to stay connected to you at all times by touching you, or touching someone who is touching you.
4 Lay the six pieces of paper on the ground around the "Vine," with the writing side up. Some of them should be only a couple of feet away from the "Vine;" others should be ten or twelve feet away.
5 Before beginning the game, say to the students, "In this week's lesson, we learned that we need to stay connected to Jesus and what he says. Today we're going to play a game where we have to stay connected like a vine stays connected to its branches."
6 To begin the game, have the students form a single file line. Have one student stand with one hand touching the "Vine" person. Tell him that he must always keep that hand on the Vine. Have him reach out his free hand and grab the hand of the next student, who will clasp hands with another, and so on until they have formed a human chain anchored by the Vine.
7 Now tell the students, "This verse from today's lesson has been broken into six pieces. Your task, as a group, is to pick up those pieces and pass them one at a time to the Vine, but you all have to keep on holding hands, the whole time."
8 Explain to the students that the person touching the Vine will make **one** motion at a time showing how the task can be completed. Each time he makes a motion, the student holding that student's hand must then make the exact same motion. Each student "passes" the motion on to the next student in line, using only his body (no words), until the student at the end of the line has received the motion and obeys it.
   [EXAMPLE: if the paper is on the ground, the student closest to the Vine could first crouch down. The student holding his hand should then crouch too, and so should the next student, and so on, until the final student has crouched. Next the vine student could reach out his hand, and so on.]
9 When a piece of paper is picked up, the blindfolded student who picks it up should "pass" it back up the chain of students. They should pass it from hand to hand all the way back to the Vine (while still holding hands).
10 When all the pieces of paper are collected, allow the students to release each other's hands. Have them gather around you and help you put the pieces of the verse in the correct order.

Psalm 23, Part III

Materials

- Psalm 23, Part III (Student Page 133 or 135, depending on which version you're using)

Directions

1 Tear out the Student Page (133 or 135) with the version of Psalm 23 you will be using.
2 Say to the student, "We've been learning Psalm 23 together. Let's say the part we've learned so far, twice." Say, together with the student, the first 2/3 of the Psalm (up through "they comfort me.")
3 Beginning with "You prepare a table before me . . ." teach the student the verses, having her repeat each phrase four times before moving on to the next one. Give any necessary help; this is a large section and may be a challenge.
4 Be sure to praise the student for working on the verses and learning them. Review the entire psalm each day for the next several days, and encourage the child to decorate the student page with a scene from the psalm.

Coloring Page

The Fruitful Vine

Jesus said that his followers should stay connected to him like branches stay connected with a grapevine. Just like the vine gives the branches the nutrients they need, Jesus gives us what we need to trust him and obey what he says.

Nature Hike

· ·

________ A seed

________ A sprout

________ A seedling

________ A young tree

________ An old tree

________ A dead tree on the ground

________ A dead tree still standing

________ A tree that is living, but with many dead branches still attached

________ A strong, living tree that is standing

________ A tree recently knocked over or cut down

________ A tree stump

________ Tree roots sticking out of the ground

________ A vine

Psalm 23, Part III (KJV)

The Lord is my shepherd; I shall not want.

He maketh me to lie down in green pastures;

He leadeth me beside the still waters;

He restoreth my soul.

He leadeth me in paths of righteousness for his name's sake.

Yea, though I walk through the valley of the shadow of death,

I will fear no evil, for thou art with me.

Thy rod and thy staff, they comfort me.

Thou preparest a table before me, in the presence of mine
  enemies.

Thou anointest my head with oil;

My cup overflows.

Surely goodness and mercy will follow me all the days of my life,

And I will dwell in the house of the Lord forever.

Psalm 23, Part III
(New International Version)

The Lord is my shepherd, I shall not be in want.

He makes me lie down in green pastures,

He leads me beside quiet waters, he restores my soul.

He guides me in paths of righteousness for his name's sake.

Even though I walk through the valley of the shadow of death,

I will fear no evil, for you are with me. Your rod and your staff,
    they comfort me.

You prepare a table before me in the presence of my enemies.

You anoint my head with oil; my cup overflows.

Surely goodness and love will follow me all the days of my life,

And I will dwell in the house of the Lord forever.

John 15:1–8
The Fruitful Vine

Unit 4

The Sermon on the Mount

Lesson 16: Give to the Needy, But Don't Show Off

Activities

Put It Into Practice Activity: **Do Good Deeds Secretly**
Craft Project: **Blow a Shofar Horn to Announce Your Good Deeds**
Activity: **Keep a Secret From Your Left Hand**
Coloring Page: **Helping Quietly**

Put It Into Practice Activity

. . . .

Do Good Deeds Secretly

Materials

- Paper
- Pencil

Directions

1. Help the student brainstorm about ways to help members of the family, or neighbors. Jot down on paper different tasks that he could do without being noticed.
   Family Examples: a load of laundry folded or put away, a sibling's chores done for him or her, toys put away, the table being set for dinner, the pet being fed or walked.
   Neighbor Example [to be done with parental supervision]: pick up trash that has blown into the neighbor's yard.
2. Have the student pick as many as desired to complete, at a time when the recipient(s) of the helpful deed are not around. Encourage the student not to draw attention to the completed work, but *you* should praise the student. Discuss how Jesus wants us to do good things because they are good and because God wants us to, not just so that we will be recognized by other people.

Blow a Shofar Horn to Announce Your Good Deeds

In this week's lesson Jesus says, "So when you give to the needy, do not announce it with trumpets, as the hypocrites do in the synagogues and on the streets." The shofar, one variety of horn that was used in Jesus' time, was made of a ram's horn. Make your own shofar—ram not required—and use it to show how annoying it can be for someone to trumpet every one of their good deeds.

Materials

- Plastic party horn/noisemaker or blower, or a kazoo
- One paper towel tube (optional: two tubes)
- Scissors
- Masking tape
- OPTIONAL: Craft paint in brown, white, tan, or black (you can choose one or more colors)
- OPTIONAL: Paintbrush
- OPTIONAL: Cup of water

Directions

1. Tell the student that a shofar is like a trumpet, but it is made from the horn of a ram or goat. There is a small hole at the narrow end that you blow through, and the air comes out the larger hole at the end of the horn.
2. If you have a party blower, remove the decorative pieces from the white plastic horn (the noise-making piece).
3. Help the student use the scissors to cut a line down the length of the paper towel tube (note that it now looks like a fruit roll-up).
4. Have the student re-roll the paper towel tube so there is one narrow end and one open end, like a cone. Before it is rolled as tightly as possible, drop the plastic horn or kazoo into the larger end of the tube so that the part you blow on is sticking out the narrow end. If you have a kazoo, make sure the circle on the kazoo is inside the paper towel tube.
5. Have the student wrap masking tape around the middle of the tube so it retains its cone shape.
6. If the plastic horn or kazoo is not already being held in place by the tightness of the rolled tube, have the student secure it with tape.
7. (OPTIONAL) To make the shofar longer, have the student cut the second paper towel tube like the first, and roll it the same way but not as tightly. Without taping the second tube beforehand, have the student slide the narrow end of the second tube into the open end of the first tube. Have the student wrap tape around the seam between the two tubes.
8. (OPTIONAL) Traditionally, shofarot (the plural of shofar) are not painted, but they can be carved. But this shofar needs a little paint to help it look more realistic. Let the student use the paint colors and paintbrush to make the shofar look like a real animal horn.
9. If you painted the shofar, let it dry.

10 Once it is complete, ask the student to blow the horn whenever he does something nice or helpful. You could, for example, ask him to clean his room. Then, every time he puts away any single item in the room, have him blow his horn. When you hear the horn, run into the room and have him tell you what he did ("I put away my socks!"). Or he could set the table for dinner, blowing the horn after placing each and every utensil/dish.

11 After the student has been doing this for a while, take the horn back from the student. (Clean off the mouthpiece, if you'd like to.) Now, you the instructor should blow the shofar whenever you do any small task. "I opened the peanut butter jar!" "I turned off the light switch!" "I picked up one sock off the floor!" etc. Find as many excuses as possible to blow the horn, and make sure you are near the student so that he hears you loud and clear.

12 After you've done this long enough for it to be annoying to the hearers, say to the student: "Did you notice how the sound became annoying and you didn't want me to blow the horn so much? That is how it is when people try to get attention for every good thing they do. God wants us to do good things for people because it's right, not to be noticed by everyone else."

Activity

. . . .

Keep a Secret From Your Left Hand

Jesus says that when you give to the needy, "Don't let your left hand know what your right hand is doing, so that your giving may be in secret." Do this activity to help the student understand that expression and to practice secret acts of kindness.

Materials

- Coloring Page from this lesson (Student Page 145)
- Pencil
- Two pieces of blank paper
- Pillowcase or light piece of cloth

Directions

1 Tell the student to look at the coloring page from this lesson. Then have him draw the same picture on another piece of paper. He can continue to look at the coloring page as a reference.

2 Once the student has finished her picture, have him point out the similarities between the two pictures (his and the original).

3 Tell the student you are going to challenge him. Take away his version of the picture and give him the other blank piece of paper. Then take away the original coloring page. Tell the student he must draw the picture again, but this time from memory. And to make it even more difficult, have him hold the pencil over his paper and then drape his hand and the paper with the pillowcase so he can't see what he is drawing.

4 When he tells you he is finished, examine his new picture and compare it to the first one he drew. Why was the second picture such a challenge? (Because he had to remember the picture details and he couldn't even see what he was doing.) Tell him, "I am guessing

you had no idea what this picture would come out looking like, because you couldn't see through the fabric. It was like your drawing hand was keeping a secret from the rest of your body! Jesus said to do your giving in secret, so secret that your left hand would not even know what your right hand is doing."

5 Tell the student that it is hard to do a kind deed for people in your family without being noticed, because they are the people that you are around most of the time. Challenge the student to do three secret acts of kindness today for members of his family (make bed, put away shoes, make them a snack, etc.). Check in with him at bedtime or see if he was able to do all three deeds without being detected! Remind him that even if no one saw him or even noticed what he did for them, God saw it all.

Memory Work

Psalm 23

Remember to review Psalm 23 this week.

Coloring Page

Helping Quietly

Both of these people are giving food to those who need it, but one person is trying to get everyone's attention, and one is helping quietly. Jesus said that when we do kind deeds for others, we shouldn't try to get everyone's attention and impress everyone with how nice we are. God sees the good things we do, and that is what matters most.

Matthew 6:1-4
Helping Quietly

Lesson 17: You Cannot Serve God and Another

Activities

Science Activity: **Earthly Treasure Doesn't Last**
Group Game: **Serving Two Masters**
Game: **Treasure Hunt**
Coloring Page: **Treasures That Don't Last**

Science Activity

Earthly Treasure Doesn't Last

This activity demonstrates to the student the rust which Jesus speaks of in today's lesson, showing one way in which earthly treasure doesn't last.

Materials

- A piece of soft white sandwich bread
- Small plastic plate
- Black marker
- S.O.S. or Brillo pad (S.O.S. works best for this activity)
- Small plastic bowl
- Vinegar (approximately 1 cup)

Directions

1. Show the student the piece of bread. Point out that it looks like a good piece of bread that someone could eat. Talk with the student about other great things to eat. Ask her to name her favorite food. With the marker, have her carefully draw a picture of her favorite food on the piece of bread.
2. Put the bread on the plate. Have the student dribble some water on the bread so it is moist (but not disintegrating). Help the student find a dark, warm place to set the bread (like inside a pot on top of the refrigerator).
3. Give the student the S.O.S. pad to examine. Ask her if she knows what it is made of (metal). Let her rinse all the blue soap out of it (this is fun). While she is rinsing,

brainstorm about all the things she likes that are made of metal or have metal in them (cars, toys, coins, jewelry, etc.).

4   Have the student put the S.O.S. pad in the bowl. Help her pour enough vinegar to almost cover the S.O.S. pad, but leave some of it exposed to the air. Set the bowl in a place where you don't mind the scent of vinegar (like the garage).

5   Check back on the bread and the S.O.S. pad after a few days. What has happened? (Mold has grown on the bread and the S.O.S. pad has rusted.) Ask her if the bread looks like it is still good to eat. (No!) Tell her that the rust has eaten away at the metal in the S.O.S. pad. (Metal bridges have collapsed because of the corrosive power of rust!) Tell her, "Things on earth don't last. Don't let them be more important to you than loving God and loving others."

Group Game

· ·

Serving Two Masters

In this week's lesson, Jesus said that it's impossible to serve God and serve something else at the same time. Those who try to do so will end up serving one master or the other. This group game illustrates the difficulty of obeying two different masters at once.

Materials

- Two sheets of paper
- Pencil

Directions

1   <u>Before class</u>, use the pencil to write orders on the two sheets of paper. Be sure to write legibly.

On the first paper, write the following orders:
1. Stand on one foot
2. Sit down on the ground
3. Wave one hand in the air
4. Wave both hands in the air
5. Flap your arms like a bird's wings
6. Hop up and down on one foot and say "Boing Boing Boing"
7. Rub your stomach and pat your head at the same time
8. Say "Hippopotamus" while turning in a circle twice
9. Do seven jumping jacks
10. Turn your head all the way around and look at the back of your shirt

On the second paper, write the following orders:
1. Hop up and down on one foot
2. Take a small hop forward
3. Take a small hop backward
4. Touch your toes with your fingers, twice
5. Lie down on your back and run in place

6. Say "Rumplestiltzkin!" five times, while jumping up and down

7. Take both of your shoes off

8. Put both of your shoes on

9. Clap your hands behind your back ten times

10. Jump as high as you can

2   You will be one of the "masters." Select a student (preferably a good reader) or an adult (if an adult is present) to be the other "master." You and the other master should stand apart from the rest of the students. Since this is an active game, make sure the students have plenty of space to wave arms, etc.

3   Say to the students, "We are your masters and you have to do what we say. Each of us will give a command, and you have to do it. Then the other master will give a command, and you have to do that one too. Do them as quickly as you can."

4   Read the first command aloud; then after the students have had a few seconds to obey, the other master reads his first command aloud. Do this for all the commands. As you go, begin to speed up (leave less and less time between the reading of the commands).

5   Say to the students, "Trying to obey two sets of directions at once was hard, wasn't it? Was it easy at the beginning? Was it harder at the end?" Then say, "In this week's lesson, Jesus told us that we can't obey two masters at once—it's impossible to put God first and put yourself first at the same time, just like it was impossible to obey two sets of orders at the same time."

Game

Treasure Hunt

Do a scavenger hunt to find ways to store up heavenly treasure—and then decide what to do with the earthly treasure (coins) the student also finds.

Materials

- Heavenly Treasure Clues (Student Page 151)
- Scissors
- Sharpie marker
- 6 empty plastic Easter eggs
- 6 dimes, quarters, OR dollar bills

Directions

1   ADVANCE SETUP (do not let the student see this): Use a Sharpie to number each egg 1 through 6. Cut apart the Heavenly Treasure Clues on Student Page 151. Place a coin or dollar in each egg, along with the clue with the corresponding number. Now hide the eggs in these places:

Egg 1: Somewhere in the bathtub area

Egg 2: Under the student's pillow

Egg 3: In the drawer where you keep the spoons

Egg 4: In the student's car seat

Egg 5: Behind the student's Bible

Egg 6: In the Student's sock drawer

Hide the eggs so they are not in plain sight, so that the student has to hunt around a little. *NOTE: These hiding places and clues have been designed for a home setting, but you can do a scavenger hunt anywhere. Just cross out the clues we provided and write your own.*

2 Now tell the student that you have hidden plastic eggs around the house. Each egg contains a way to store up heavenly treasure and a piece of earthly treasure. Say to the student, "To find the first treasure, go to the place you need to be when you're dirty."

3 Go with the student as she finds the clues. You can hold onto the clues and the money she finds. Once she has finished finding all the eggs, bring everything back to a table.

4 Set the money aside. Read each suggestion about how to store up heavenly treasure. Help the student brainstorm about specific ways she could carry these out:

Give to the poor. (What organizations do you know that do this?)

Visit the sick or lonely. (Are there any hospitals or nursing homes in your area? Do you know anyone who is homebound?)

Love your family. (What are some ways you can show that love?)

Help out at your church. (Are there ways the student can volunteer?)

Pray for someone in need. (Think about people you know who need prayer and then stop and pray for them now!)

5 Now bring the pile of money closer. Ask the student how you and she can use this earthly treasure to help others. (Some ideas: Donate the money to your church or a nonprofit organization; use the money to purchase art supplies to make cards or crafts to give out at a nursing home or hospital; purchase a small gift like flowers to bless someone who could use a pick-me-up.) Then go and do it!

Memory Work

Psalm 23

Remember to review Psalm 23 this week.

Coloring Page

Treasures That Don't Last

Jesus says that sooner or later earthly treasures will either rot, crumble, be eaten by bugs, or be stolen by someone. But heavenly treasures never rot or get stolen because heavenly treasures are the things that we do to serve God—like giving to the needy, being kind to people around us, or loving our families.

Heavenly Treasure Clues

Give to the poor.

*To find the next clue,
go to the place where
you rest your head.*

Visit the sick or lonely.

*To find the next clue,
find what you need
to eat soup.*

Love your family.

*To find the next clue,
go to the place where
you must buckle yourself.*

Help out at your church.

*To find the next clue,
go to the place where
you can read God's Words.*

Do something kind for your neighbors.

*To find the next clue,
find what you need to put on
when you have cold feet.*

Pray for someone in need.

*Congratulations!
You have found
all the treasure!*

Matthew 6:19–24
Treasures That Don't Last

Lesson 18: Be Honest With Yourself Before You Judge

Activities

Game: **Plank in Your Eye**
Game: **What Do I Have?**
Memory Work: **Say Psalm 23 to an Audience**
Coloring Page: **Speck and Plank**

Game

Plank in Your Eye

This silly and goopy activity will help the student remember that when we ignore our own faults, it is like having planks in our eyes. We can't see anything the right way.

Materials

- Peach
- Sharpie marker
- At least 10 craft sticks (some students will love using lots more!)
- Plate

Directions

1 Give the student the peach and have him draw two giant eyes on it with the Sharpie.
2 Tell the student that he should pretend that the peach eyes are looking for something small in the room. Play a few rounds of "I Spy . . ." where the student's peach eyes say "I Spy with my Eyes something that is [color]." You are the guesser.
3 Tell the student, "Those eyes can see well. But what if our peach has some faults that he ignores and doesn't want to fix? Those faults are like planks." Holding the peach over a plate to catch the drips, let the student poke the craft sticks into his peach eyes. Let him use as many as he wants.
4 After some sticks are stuck in the peach, ask the student, "How well do you think the eyes can see now?" Tell the student that the only way to remove these planks is to ask God to show you your faults, forgive you for them, and help you change for the better.

What Do I Have?

Materials

- An array of everyday items; books, toys, fruit, etc. The number of each item must be equal to the number of players, i.e. with two players there must be two books, two bananas, two toy cars, etc. The items don't have to be identical, just similar.
- A blindfold for each player

Directions

1   Blindfold each player. Put the items in a row in front of them, each row of items in the same order.
2   Say "Go!" Each player must start at the beginning of the row of items and pick up each one. Each player must identify what he has in his hands by touch only, without looking. When the player thinks he knows what the item is, he shouts it out. If the player correctly identifies the item, both players move to the next item and the player who identified it gets a point. If the player is wrong, the other player gets a point and both players stay on that item until someone correctly identifies it.
3   If there is more than one other player, everyone gets a point except the person who incorrectly identified the item. So, if there are four players and they are each holding a toy car, and one of them says "It's a banana!" all the players except him get a point, and they keep guessing until someone says "toy car."
4   At the end of the row of items, whoever has the most points wins.

Say Psalm 23 to an Audience

Materials

- Another person (preferably not the instructor) to whom the student can say this memorized psalm

Directions

1   Say to the student, "These past few weeks, you have been learning Psalm 23, a poem about how God takes care of us like a shepherd cares for his sheep. In a moment, we're going to say this psalm out loud for [name of person]. But first, let's review it to keep it in your memory. Remember that it starts with 'The Lord is my shepherd.' Let's say that together now."
2   Together, say the psalm, a verse or two at a time.
3   Now have the student say the psalm to another person besides you. Stand near the student and give help if necessary. Give lots of praise and encouragement.

. . . .

The Speck and the Plank

This girl is trying to take the speck out of her friend's eye, but she can't see the huge plank of wood in her own eye. Jesus said that's what it's like, when we try to correct someone before checking to see where we might be wrong too.

Matthew 7:1–5
The Speck and the Plank

Lesson 19: Living a Disciplined Life

Activities

Activity: "Broad and Narrow Paths" Maze
Coloring Page: The Narrow Path

Activity
• •
"Broad and Narrow Paths" Maze

Materials

- Pencil
- "Broad and Narrow Paths" Maze (Student Page 163)

Directions

1 Tear out Student Page 163.
2 Say to the student, "In today's lesson, we learned that following Jesus is not always easy. Sometimes, doing what Jesus says is not like walking a nice, smooth, wide road. Sometimes it is like walking a difficult path that's hard to find. Now we are going to do a maze that has broad paths and narrow paths. Can you find your way from one end to the other? Be careful; the path is not easy to see."
3 Let the student try to find her way, with the pencil, from "Start" to "Finish." Give hints if necessary, but it is all right for her to struggle with the broad and narrow paths a little bit. That's part of the point of the activity.

Coloring Page
• •
The Narrow Path

Traveling through the small gate and walking the narrow road means doing what Jesus wants you to do, even if it is hard. If you do what is right, even if it is hard, you will learn to know God better and better. Following Jesus is sometimes a harder road to take, but it is always the better road.

Maze: Broad and Narrow Paths

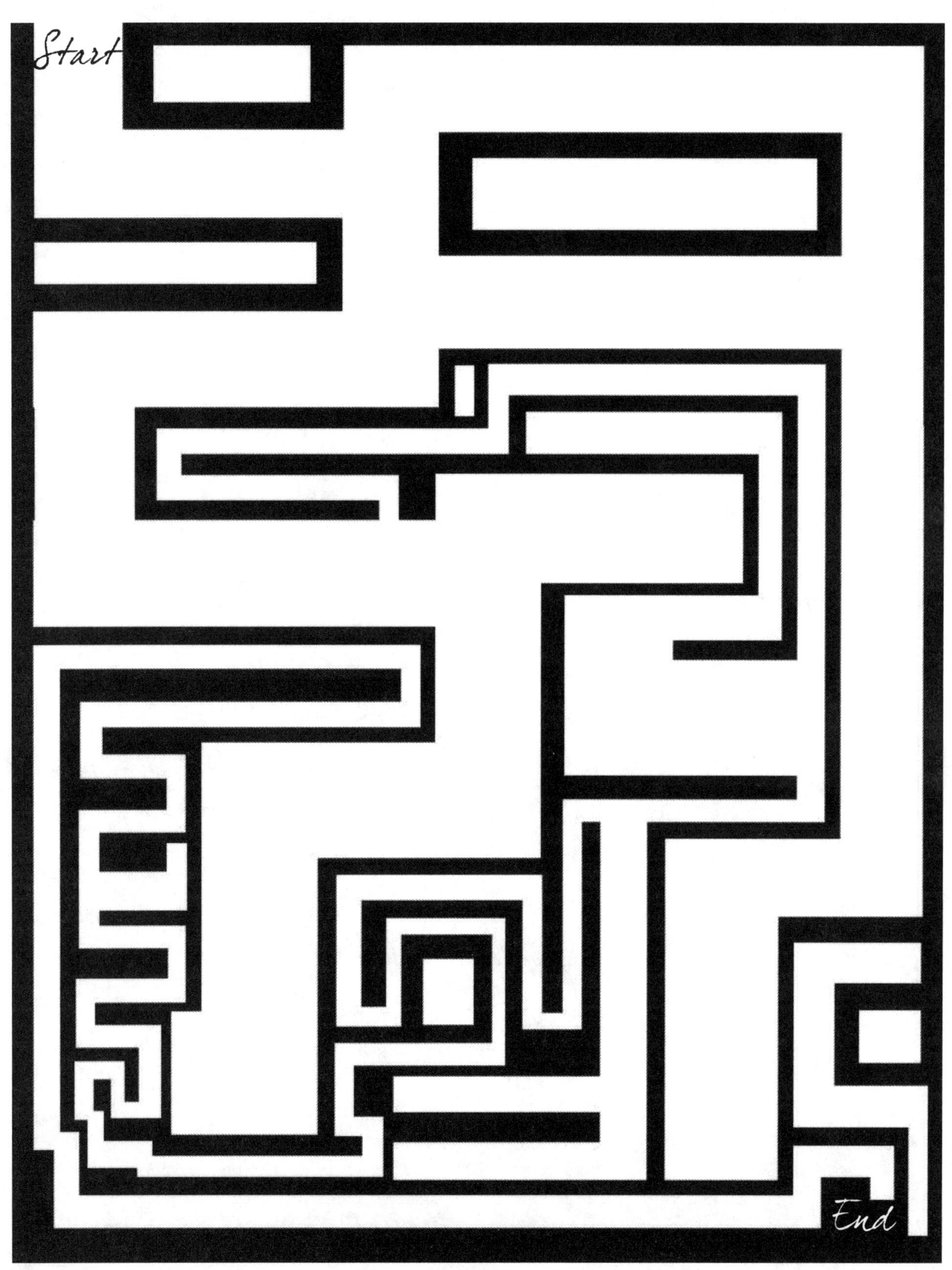

Matthew 7:13–14
The Narrow Door and the Narrow Path

Lesson 20: Bad Trees Always Bear Bad Fruit

Activities

Game: **Good Tree Board Game**
Craft Project: **Design a "Good Trees" T-Shirt**
Coloring Page: **Good Fruit, and Bad Leaders in Disguise**

Game

· ·

Good Tree Board Game

This game can be played with one or two students.

Materials

- Good Tree game board, Student Pages 171 and 173
- 8.5" by 11" piece of cardboard (for mounting the game board)
- Good Tree / Bad Tree playing cards (tree images), Student Page 175
- Good Tree / Bad Tree playing cards (descriptions), Student Page 177
- Crayons, markers, or colored pencils
- Scissors
- Glue
- Colored candies such as Skittles or M&M's to use as game pieces

Directions

1 Remove the game board from Pages 171 and 173 in the Activity Book, along the perforation lines. Instruct the student to color the tree with lots of bright colors, but try to make sure that he doesn't cover up the "path" of leaves.

2 Tear out the Good Tree/Bad Tree playing cards and descriptions on Page 175 and Page 177. Have the student color in the tree images on the playing cards. Then glue the back of the tree image page to the back of the descriptions page, making sure that the tops of the pages line up, and the playing card grid lines up.

3 Next, cut out the playing cards. (Each card should have a tree image on one side, and a description on the other side.)

4   Set up the game: Have each player place his "game piece" (the candy) at the Start. Shuffle the playing cards, and then stack them to the side of the game board, with the descriptions facing UP.

5   To play: Draw the top playing card, being careful to cover the image on the back with your hand. Read the description to the first player. That student must then guess "good tree" or "bad tree," according to whether the type of "fruit" described in the scenario is good or bad. The back of the card will show a good, fruitful tree, or a bad tree with no leaves or fruit. If he guesses correctly, then he may move the game piece the number of spaces designated on the back of the card. If not, the game piece remains where it is. It is then the next player's turn.

6   The object of the game is to be the first player to reach any one of the pieces of fruit.

Craft Project

Design a "Good Trees" T-Shirt

Materials

- Bleach gel pen (available at grocery stores)
- Solid-colored T-Shirt (a brighter color is best, but not white or black)
- Thick piece of cardboard, 1 square foot
- OPTIONAL: water soluble marker

Directions

1   Place the piece of cardboard inside the T-shirt (so that the bleach will not bleed through more than one layer at a time) and lay it on a flat surface.

2   Using the bleach gel pen, have the student draw a "fruit tree" design on the front of the T-shirt. Encourage him to make it a large, but simple design, with widely spaced lines because the bleached-out colors may run a little bit. The bleach will take a few minutes to show up properly; tell the student not to re-trace his lines if he doesn't see them show up right away. (If the student has trouble, draw a design for him using the water soluble marker, and let him trace your design with the bleach pen.)

3   Let the T-shirt sit for about ten minutes or until the bleached color begins to show beneath the gel, allowing the bleach-design to dry thoroughly. Don't allow the bleach to dry for too long; it may begin to run.

4   Remove the cardboard and set it aside. Rinse out the T-shirt in cold water in the sink.

5   Then put the T-shirt through your cold-rinse cycle in your washing machine. Dry the T-shirt. Once the design is dry, have the student flip over the T-shirt with the cardboard inside.

6   Have the student use the bleach gel pen to write part of this verse from this week's lesson on the back of the T-shirt: "Good trees bear good fruit." [Quotation from Matthew 7:18]

7   When all of the bleach lines have shown up and the T-shirt has dried, wash the shirt to rid it of any residual bleach. (The first time you wash the T-shirt, wash it separately from other clothing.)

Good Fruit, and Bad Leaders in Disguise

Some leaders pretend to speak for God but they are really leading people in ways that they shouldn't go. Jesus said these people are like dangerous wolves dressed up like harmless sheep, or like nice-looking trees that produce rotten fruit.

Good Tree Game Board

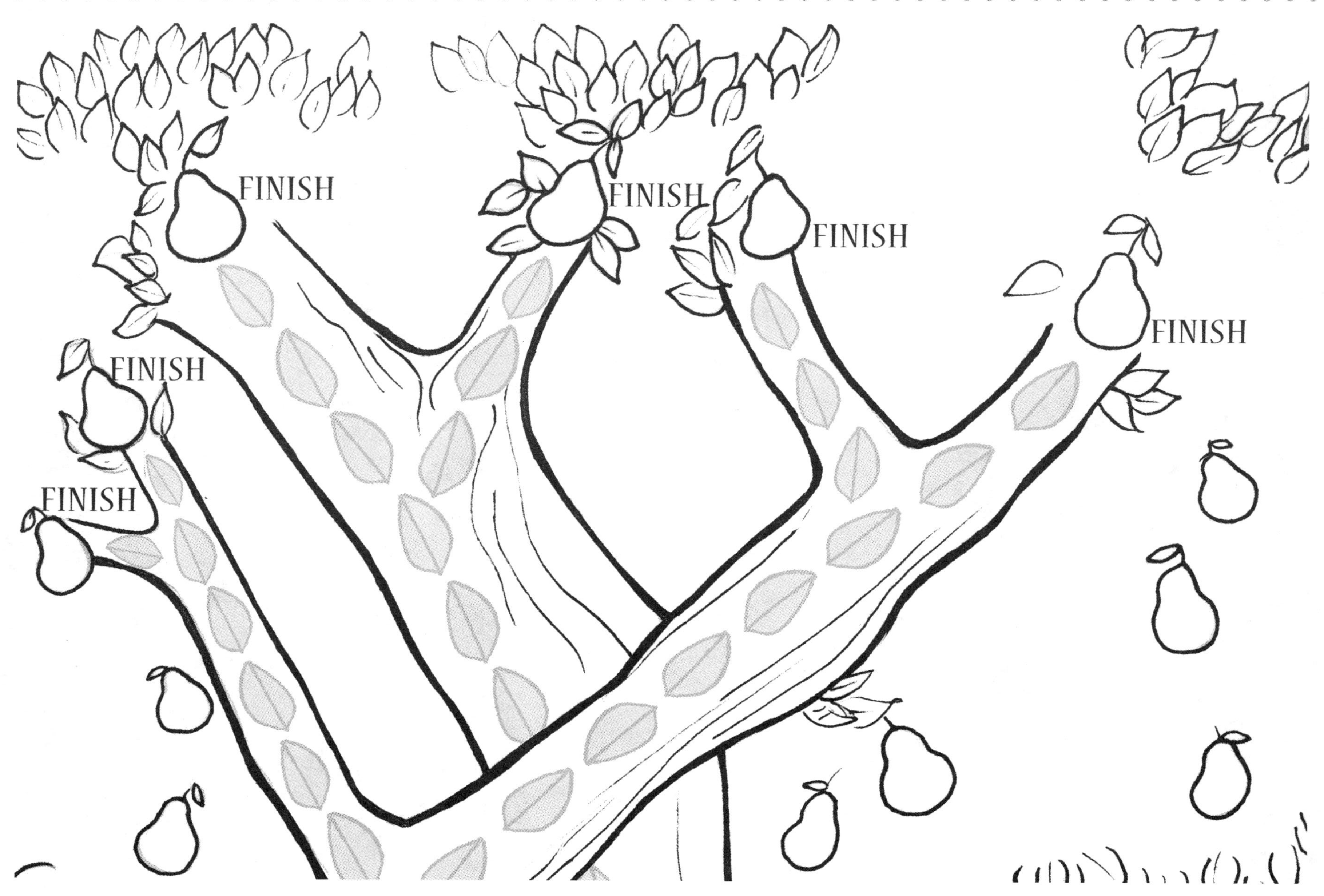

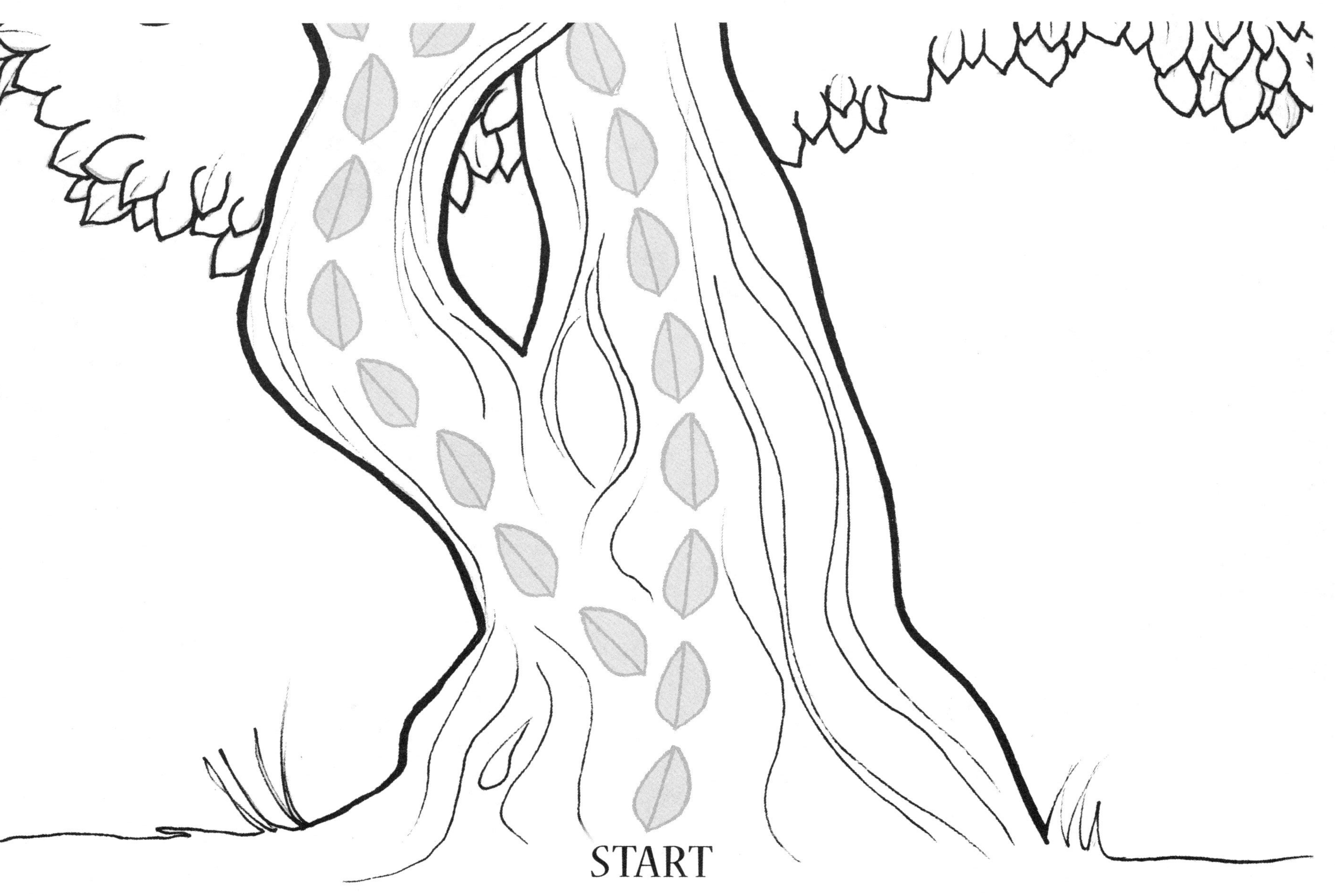

START

Good Tree/Bad Tree Playing Cards

1 space 	2 spaces 	1 space 	2 spaces 
3 spaces 	4 spaces 	2 spaces 	3 spaces 
5 spaces 	2 spaces 	3 spaces 	4 spaces 
4 spaces 	3 spaces 	3 spaces 	2 spaces 

Good Tree/Bad Tree Playing Cards

Your mother asks if you cleaned your room, and you say, "Yes." But really, you just put all your things under a sheet.	You get angry and hit your friend on the head.	You see a new child at church, and you talk to him and let him sit next to you.	You say something kind to your friend.
The new student at school asks to play with you at recess and you push him away.	Your mom told you it's not time for cookies. You take cookies from the pantry and put them in your pocket for "later."	You see a person who is injured, and you run to find an adult to help out.	Without being asked to help, you lend a hand when your sister or brother is cleaning up their toys.
You knock over a stack of books (by accident), and when the teacher says, "Who did this?", you say, "I don't know."	Your brother or sister takes the toy you were playing with, so you grab it back out of their hands.	When someone forgets to bring their lunch to school, you share yours with them.	You knock over a stack of books (by accident), and when the teacher says, "Who did this?", you say, "It was me."
You run across the street after your parents told you not to go.	While the teacher at church is teaching the Bible lesson, you keep talking loudly and nobody can hear the teacher.	You wait patiently for your turn to swing on the swingset.	Your friend breaks your toy, but then says that she's sorry. You say, "I forgive you."

Matthew 7:15–23
Bad Leaders and Good Fruit

Unit 5
Jesus' Early Life

Lesson 21: God Is on the Move...Again

Activities

Craft Project: **Make a High Priest's Breastplate**
Group or Individual Game: **Take a Vow of Silence**
Activity: **"The Angel's Announcement" Word Search**
Coloring Page: **Zechariah Has Seen an Angel**

Craft Project

. . . .

Make a High Priest's Breastplate

Materials

- Piece of cardboard, 7" x 9"
- Oven-bake clay such as Sculpey (available at craft stores or at online retailers such as Amazon; alternately you can use colored construction paper, or white paper that you then color)
- Watercolor paints, water, and paint brushes (if using clay)
- Long sash of cloth (1–2 inches wide)
- Cookie sheet or baking sheet

Directions

1   Say to the student, "In this lesson you learned about the priests in the time just before Jesus' birth. You learned that they worked in the Temple, took care of the sacrifices, gave blessings, made sure things were in the proper place, lit lamps and burned incense. The priest who was in charge, called the High Priest, wore special clothing, and today we're going to make part of that clothing, a breastplate."
2   Help the student cut the piece of cardboard in a rectangular shape that will cover the front of the student's torso (from collarbone to belly button). In each of the four corners, help her cut a hole large enough to thread the sash of cloth through.
3   Draw an outline half an inch in from the edge of the cardboard, all the way around the inside of the border, forming a rectangle within the rectangle.
4   Have the student help you break the clay into 12 equal pieces and form them into oval-shaped disks (roughly two inches tall and one inch wide) with the flat side face down on the baking sheet. They should look like twelve domes on a baking sheet. These will be

the "jewels" on your breastplate. The 12 stones represented the 12 tribes of Israel, according to Exodus 28:15–21.

5   Put the oval-shaped disks on the baking sheet, and bake them in the oven according to package directions. When they are cool, it will be time to paint them. Paint the stones in the following colors and place them on the breastplate in this order:

red	pale green	deep red
green	deep blue	white
dull red	grey	purple
bluish green	bluish white	green

6   After the stones are painted, let them dry. Glue them to the inside rectangle of the breastplate, in the order shown in the diagram.

7   After the stones are glued to the breastplate and the glue has dried, thread your sash through the top two holes, running the sash across the top back of the breastplate. Place the breastplate on your student's chest and put the two ends of the sash over each shoulder. Criss-cross the ends across his back and bring around his waist to the front bottom corners of the breast plate. Thread each end of the sash through one hole. Bring the ties back around to the back and tie.

Group or Individual Game

Take a Vow of Silence

This game can be played with one student or with a group.

Materials

- A timer with at least a 30-minute capacity
- Ten items to use as rewards (candies, pennies, etc)
- OPTIONAL Group Material: one piece of paper per team of students

Directions

1   Say to the student, "In this week's lesson, the angel Gabriel was sent by God to tell Zechariah that he would have a son. But Zechariah didn't believe that this could happen. So the angel also told Zechariah that he would not be able to speak until the child was born. Zechariah wasn't able to speak until a week after the baby was born, when the family gave the baby a name. This was probably a period of at least 41–43 weeks that he was silent. That's like being quiet from Christmas, all the way through the winter, all through the spring, and all through the summer. Do you think this was hard for him? Do you

think he used writing or hand signs to communicate with people? Today, we are going to play a game where you try to remain silent for as long as possible. Do you think it will be hard, or easy?"

2   Pick an amount of time for the student or students to be silent. Fifteen to twenty minutes might be a realistic time for 2nd graders; older children can last longer. [For group use: divide the students into several small, equal "teams" and give each team a sheet of paper on which you have written a task, which the team must accomplish silently or with only written communication. Such tasks might include "get in a line starting with the person whose birthday is earliest in the year, and ending with the person whose birthday is latest in the year."]

3   Show the student the ten pennies or candies, etc, about one for every two minutes the student wants to be silent (longer for older children). Explain that the student may not talk for [the time span you selected]. The student may gesture and write, but cannot make any noise (including grunting/gurgling/squeaking noises!) Every time the student forgets, and speaks or makes a sound, one of the little rewards will be taken away. Any rewards left at the end of the allotted time are hers for the keeping.

4   Start the timer for the allotted time. Every time the student forgets and makes a noise, take away a reward. For maximum effect, pick a time when the student needs to interact with other people—a time when she is around the rest of the family, such as preparing dinner or doing chores. [Optional: If you have more than one student doing this at a time, try staggering the silent times for each student, so that at any given moment, everyone else is allowed to speak, but one student is not.]

5   Afterwards, talk about what was difficult about the activity. Say to the student, "Think about how hard it would be to stay quiet like that, for nine months. Do you remember why the angel made Zechariah unable to speak for this long time?" *Answer: the angel made this happen because Zechariah did not believe that God could do what he said he would do.*

Activity

• •

"The Angel's Announcement" Word Search

Materials

- "The Angel's Announcement" Word Search (Student Page 187)
- Pencil

Directions

1   Tear out Student Page 187
2   Say to the student, "Look for the words from this week's lesson that are hidden in the word search. Six of them run left to right; four of them run top to bottom."
3   If needed, help the student find the words. They are listed below the word search. Here is the answer key:

H Q P V S **H E R O D** W E O Z F
H V O S J Z W T J B F S D M N
K T O **T** P **A N G E L** T X Q V M
P R I E S T R V Y Q A V **M** P C
S Y T **M** S T Y B N F M P I K M
T O K **P** J B P H Y K C Y **R** K Z
Y M T **L** S P E C I A L S **A** X Y
M S A **E** T **G A B R I E L** C X G
F Y J Q J X H O J V K T **L** N K
U W X D **O** A X O E U L P **E** J M
R J M T **H** P M Q S I B C M N U
B I H H **N** B L G U E K D U Z W
T G S J B K C D S C K Z U B R
X K D N I K L N T S R **B A B Y**
I K I D B X P E L U Q W W F N

Coloring Page

· ·

Zechariah Has Seen an Angel

This is Zechariah, when he came out of the room in the Temple where the angel had spoken to him. He couldn't speak, just as the angel said would happen. But he knew that God was about to do something amazing!

The Angel's Announcement
Word Search

```
H Q P V S H E R O D W E O Z F
H V O S J Z W T J B F S D M N
K T O T P A N G E L T X Q V M
P R I E S T R V Y Q A V M P C
S Y T M S T Y B N F M P I K M
T O K P J B P H Y K C Y R K Z
Y M T L S P E C I A L S A X Y
M S A E T G A B R I E L C X G
F Y J Q J X H O J V K T L N K
U W X D O A X O E U L P E J M
R J M T H P M Q S I B C M N U
B I H H N B L G U E K D U Z W
T G S J B K C D S C K Z U B R
X K D N I K L N T S R B A B Y
I K I D B X P E L U Q W W F N
```

JOHN	BABY
JESUS	ANGEL
MIRACLE	PRIEST
SPECIAL	TEMPLE
GABRIEL	HEROD

Luke 1:5–25
Zechariah Cannot Speak After He Meets the Angel

Lesson 22: The Coming of the King

Activities

Craft Activity: **Announce the Coming King**
Group Game: **Waiting for the King**
Coloring Page: **The Announcement**

Craft Activity

Announce the Coming King

In this activity the student will create an announcement poster to help tell others about Jesus' birth. Use ordinary paper, or, if you and the student want to do a more elaborate craft, make "parchment" using the Make an Ancient Scroll *directions from Lesson 29, page 246–247.*

Materials

- Construction paper or ordinary unlined paper
- Art supplies to decorate the paper (crayons, markers, paint, glitter, stickers)
- OPTIONAL: if you decide to make your poster on ancient-looking "parchment," use the Materials list from "Make an Ancient Scroll," Lesson 29, page 246–247. [This "parchment" will be more fragile, so it won't be able to take as much decoration. But it will have a more ancient look.]

Directions

1   Have the student use the art supplies to make an announcement poster, telling everyone about the baby that Mary is going to have. Use the following questions to help the student create the content of the poster. The content could be presented in words or pictures or symbols (for instance, a crown could stand for "king"). If the student needs help remembering some of these details, remind him, using Luke 1:26-38 or pages 77-78 of the *Instructor Text*.

    What is going to happen to Mary very soon?
    What will the baby's name be?
    He will be like a great king from long ago. What was that old king's name?
    What will he do for people?
    How long will his kingdom last?
    Whose son will the baby be?

2   Once the announcement is complete, have the student take it to various members of his household, school, or church, and "announce" the birth of Jesus by telling them what the paper says and explaining what it means.

Group Game
· ·
Waiting For the King

This game is a variation on the card game "Spoons," and reminds the students of the people in Jesus' time who were waiting for God's special King to come.

Materials
- Deck of playing cards
- Spoons (one less spoon than the total number of players/students)

Instructions
1   Have all the students sit in a circle, with space in the middle.
2   Find all four King cards in the deck. Show the students the four King cards and say, "In today's lesson we heard about how people were waiting for a special king, sent by God. Do you see these Kings? [point to their crowns.] Watch for the King. If you see one of these cards, very quickly you should grab a spoon from the middle of the circle, and hold it up. "
3   Put three of the four Kings aside, leaving only one. Then shuffle the deck well so no one knows where the King is.
4   Place the spoons in the middle of the circle. There should always be one less spoon than the number of students.
5   You, the teacher, are the "dealer." Begin flipping through the deck, placing each card face up, in a pile in the center of the circle.
6   As soon as the students see the King card laid down, they should grab for the spoons. Anyone left without a spoon is out. That player must get up and leave the circle. The remaining students should now shrink the circle. Each time a round ends, take a different King card (so that the color/suit is different), and reshuffle the deck so that once again, one King is hidden in the deck.
7   Before each round, remove one spoon from the middle so the remaining students always outnumber the remaining spoons by one. When it's down to two students, the first one to grab the spoon when he sees the King wins the game.

Coloring Page
· ·
The Announcement

An angel called Gabriel appeared to Mary and told her that she was going to have a very special child, the Son of God. Many artists have made pictures of what this scene might have looked like. This drawing is based on a painting called *The Annunciation* by an artist named Henry Ossawa Tanner (1859–1937).

Luke 1:26–38
The Angel Gabriel Tells Mary about her Baby

Lesson 23: God Exalts the Humble

Activities

Craft Project: **Make an Illuminated *Magnificat***
Memory Work: **The *Magnificat*, Part I**
Coloring Page: **Mary and Elizabeth**

Craft Project and Memory Work
· ·
Make an Illuminated *Magnificat*

Materials

- Crayons, colored pencils, or markers
- Illuminated *Magnificat* page (Student Page 197)

Directions

1 Say to the student, "Remember that in this week's lesson, Mary sang a song of thankful-ness and praise to God. The words she spoke are famous: for hundreds of years, millions of people have learned them and sung them. The prayer-song is sometimes called the *Magnificat* [say mag-NIFF-ih-CAHT], which is the Latin word for 'magnifies.' Maybe you can see how the word "magnificat" sounds like 'magnifies.' Mary says 'My soul magnifies the Lord,' which is another way of saying 'My soul wants to tell everyone how great the Lord is.' Today we'll decorate this verse, to hang in our house."

2 Tear out Student Page 197, and show it to the student. Say, "This kind of writing is called an 'illuminated' verse. It means that the words are written in beautiful handwriting with lots of decoration."

3 (Optional) To see many wonderful examples of illuminated manuscripts, and learn more about how they were made, visit the British Library's collection online at http://www.bl.uk/catalogues/illuminatedmanuscripts/tours.asp, or the University of Louisville's collection at http://digital.library.louisville.edu/collections/mss/

4 Have the student color the decorative border, the initial "A," and anything else she would like to color on the page.

5 Hang the page in a prominent place in the home, such as on the refrigerator or in the student's room.

The *Magnificat*, Part I

Materials

- Student Page 197 from previous activity, "Make an Illuminated *Magnificat*" (see above)

Directions

1   Using the Student Page from the "Make an Illuminated *Magnificat*" activity, read these two verses to the student.
2   Say, "This is the prayer that Mary said, thanking God for what he was doing. We can use it to thank God, too. This week we will begin to learn this prayer by heart."
3   Say, "Repeat this first phrase after me three times: My soul glorifies the Lord."
4   When the student can say the first phrase, add the second. Say, "Now repeat this line three times: And my spirit rejoices in God my Savior."
5   When the student can say the second phrase, add the third. Say, "Repeat the next line three times after me: For he has been mindful of the humble state of his servant."
6   Repeat the new, combined phrases four times. Give promptings where necessary. (The student will learn the rest of the prayer next week).

Coloring Page

Mary and Elizabeth

After she found out she was going to have a baby, Mary went to see her relative Elizabeth, who was also about to have a child. When Mary greeted Elizabeth, right then Elizabeth felt her baby moving and kicking inside of her. Elizabeth understood this is not just a normal baby kick. God was telling Elizabeth that her baby and Mary's baby were both blessed by God. Both Mary and Mary's child were going to be used by God in some extraordinary way. Mary already knew this because Gabriel told her, but now Elizabeth knew too and she told Mary so.

Illuminated *Magnificat*

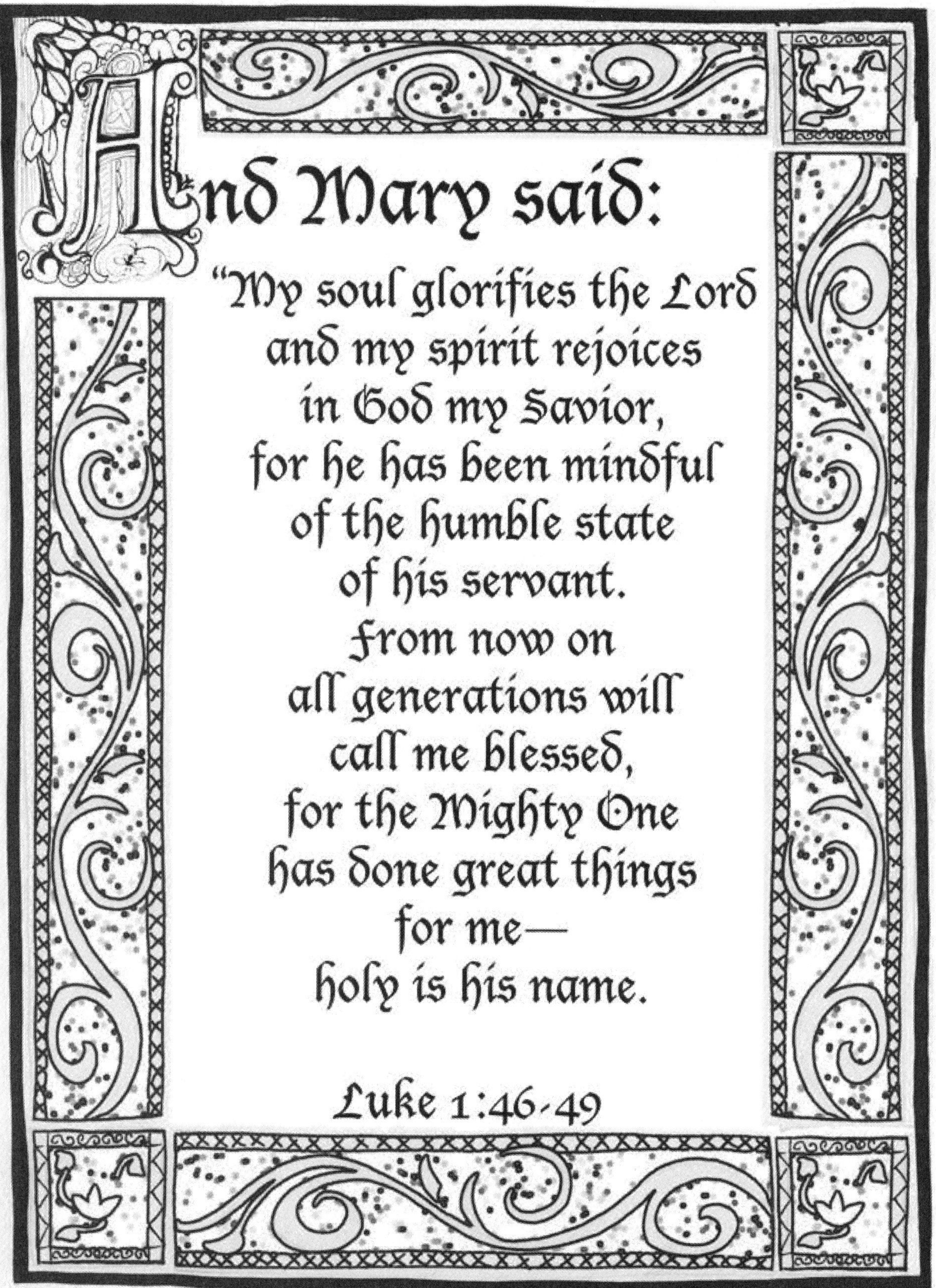

Luke 1:39–56
Elizabeth Greets Mary

Lesson 24: God is About to Rescue Israel

Activities

Activity: **Create Names On A Writing Tablet**
History Activity: **Anthroponomastics**
Memory Work: **The *Magnificat,* Part II**
Coloring Page: **Naming John**

Activity

Create Names on a Writing Tablet

Materials

- A baking pan with raised sides
- Sand (the finer the sand the better)
- 1½ to 2 cups water
- A thin stick to use as a writing tool (a toothpick or the stick of a lollipop, for instance)

Directions

1 Tell the student, "When Zechariah couldn't talk, he wrote the name of his son on his writing tablet, and everyone knew that was what his son had to be called. Today we're going to make a writing tablet and write some names on it."
2 Have the student fill the pan about with sand, to about halfway up the edge.
3 Have the student pour in about 1 ½ to 2 cups of water. The goal is for the sand to be wet, but not so wet that it's swampy. The ideal consistency is about that of sand on the beach after the wave has washed back out.
4 Give the student the toothpick/lollipop stick and bring him family members/pets/stuffed animals. Ask him what their names are. He can write whatever name he wants on his "writing tablet." For the rest of the day, everyone else has to call them whatever name the student wrote for them.

Anthroponomastics

Materials

- Pencil
- Student Page 205, Family Names
- Highlighter

Directions

1 Say to the student, "When it came time for John to be named, everyone expected a family name to be picked (such as Zechariah). A family name is a name that occurs twice or more times in a family. This often happens because children are named after someone in the family. Sometimes they will give a family member's first name to a baby as a middle name, or use someone's first name as a first name again, like when someone is named as a "Junior." People were surprised when Zechariah's baby was named John since there were no Johns in Elizabeth's and Zechariah's family."

2 Using the activity sheet, help the student find out and write down family members' names, middle names included.

3 Have the student look for names that show up more than once. Have him highlight the ones that do. This is familial anthroponomy, the study of personal names and the origins of personal names. Remind the student how, even though the name "John" had not been given to anyone else in Zechariah and Elizabeth's family before, they named this baby "John" because the angel had told them to.

Memory Work

The *Magnificat*, Part II

Materials

- Student Page 197 from the "Make an Illuminated *Magnificat*" activity in Lesson 23

Directions

1 Show Student Page 197 to the student. Say, "Last week, we learned the first half of this prayer. Today we will learn the rest. Let's say the first part first. Repeat after me: My soul glorifies the Lord, and my spirit rejoices in God my Savior. For he has been mindful of the humble state of his servant."

2 Say, "Now let's say the first new line three times together. From now on, all generations will call me blessed."

3 When the student can say that line, add the next line. Say "Repeat this line after me three times: For the Mighty One has done great things for me." *[Note: If it is helpful,*

you can add a physical motion to this line as a memory device: make an exaggerated flexing motion with your biceps on "Mighty One."]

4 Then add the final line: "Say: Let's say the last line three times together: Holy is his name."

5 When the student has mastered that line, add all the lines together. The student may not be able to do this easily; give encouragement and don't continue past the point of frustration. Review the *Magnificat* each day with the student until it is learned by heart.

Coloring Page

Naming John

When Elizabeth's baby was born, she and Zechariah named him John, as the angel had said to do. The relatives were surprised by this, since "John" was not a common name in their family, but Zechariah and Elizabeth did it anyway. Once the baby was named, Zechariah was able to speak again.

Family Names

Great Grandpa's name

Great Grandpa's name

Great Grandma's name

Great Grandma's name

Grandpa's name

Grandpa's name

Grandma's name

Grandma's name

Cousins' names

Uncles' or aunts' names

Uncles' or aunts' names

Cousins' names

Dad's name

Mom's name

My name

Brothers' or sisters' names

Luke 1:57–80
Zechariah and Elizabeth Name the Baby "John"

Unit 6

Jesus' Disciples

Lesson 25: Jesus is the Son of God

Activities

Review Activity: **Building on a Strong Foundation**
Activity: **Boat Maze**
Coloring Page: **A Strong Foundation**

Activity

• •

Building on A Strong Foundation

Materials

- Church and house templates, from Student Page 213
- Scissors
- Crayons, markers, or colored pencils
- Tape
- 8" x 11" casserole dish (or similar size)
- Small ramekin or bowl (with a flat base)
- ½ cup rice
- 2 cups water (in a measuring cup or drinking glass—just not a watering can)

Directions

1. Help the student to neatly cut out the church and house templates. She may then color the sides *without* dashed lines, as desired.
2. Fold the church and house templates along the dashed lines, keeping the lines on the interior. Tape the sides to hold them in place (see illustration to the right).
3. Place the ramekin upside-down inside the casserole dish. Put it in the left or right half, not in the center. In the other half of the casserole dish, next to the ramekin, pour the ½ cup of rice into a small mound.
4. Place the paper church on top of the ramekin (the "rock"), and the paper house on top of the rice (the "sand").

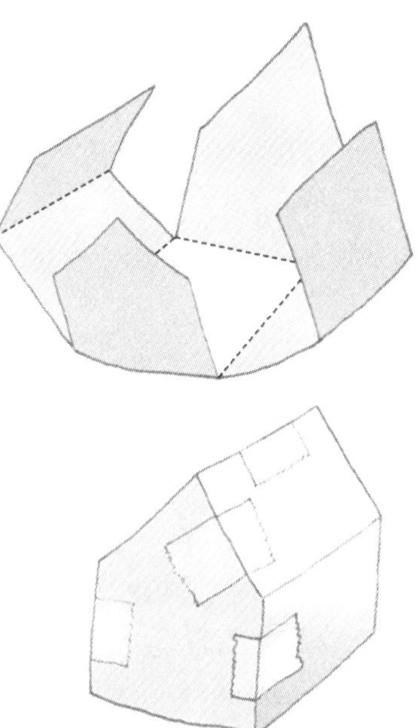

210

5 Taking the measuring cup (holding the 2 cups of water), say, "Here come the flood-waters!" Let the student pour the water into the casserole dish, all at once.
6 Observe what happens to the paper house, versus what happens to the paper church.

- Discuss with the student what it means to build something on a firm foundation, versus building something on a weak foundation.

Activity

Boat Maze

Materials

- Boat Maze (Student Page 215)
- Pencil

Directions

1 Tear out Student Page 215, containing the Boat Maze.
2 Say to the student, "This week's lesson showed Jesus' disciples learning about who Jesus was. Many of the disciples, Jesus' students who became his special helpers, started out as fishermen on the Sea of Galilee. When this story begins, Jesus and his disciples have just used a boat like this one to cross that sea."
3 Have the student use her pencil to find a way from one end of the maze to the other.

Coloring Page

A Strong Foundation

In this week's lesson, Peter said that Jesus was the Son of God, and he was right! The kingdom of heaven—from the first disciples until today—is built on the strong foundation that Jesus is the Son of God. Color this picture of a house built on a strong rock foundation.

Church and House Templates

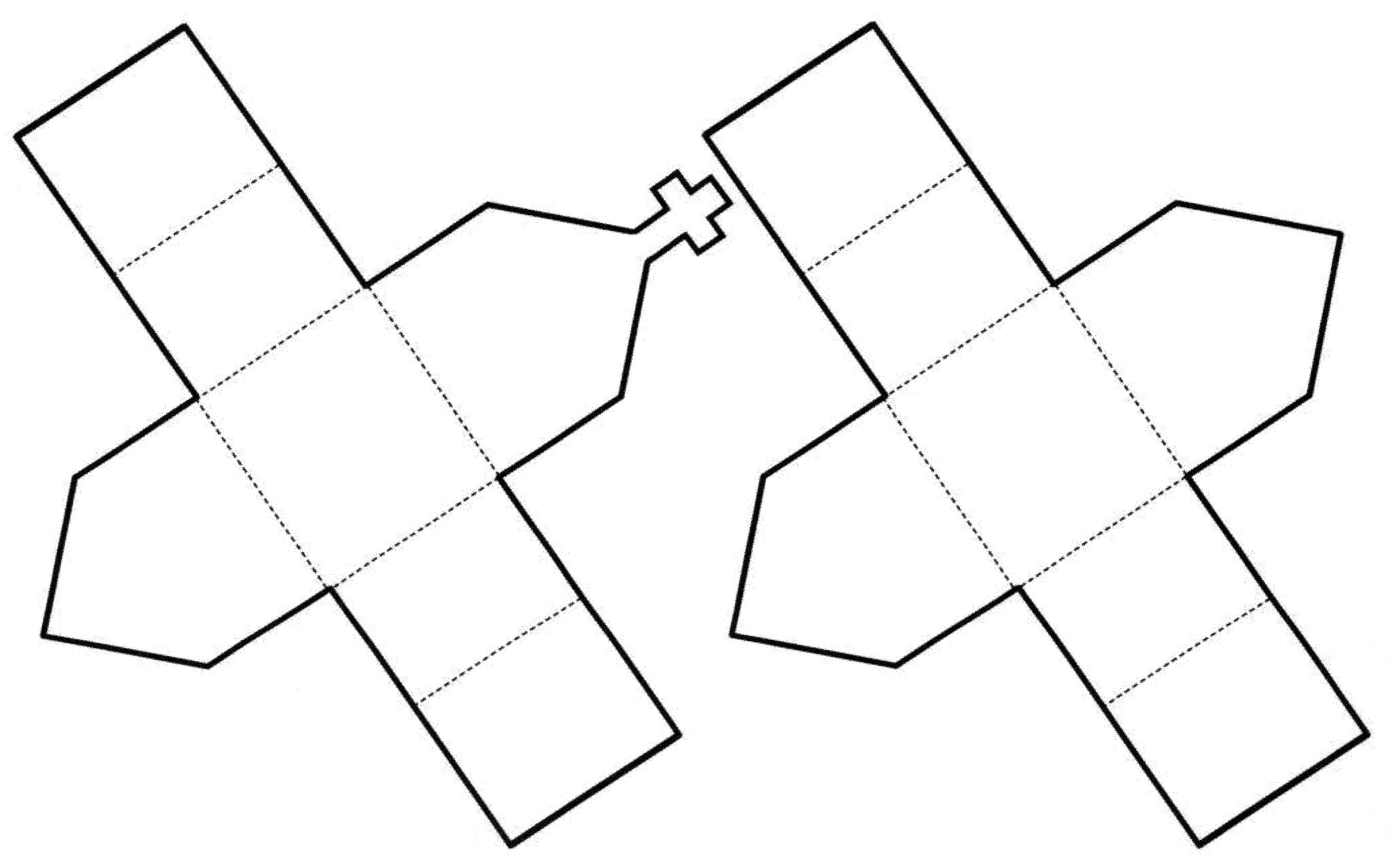

Boat Maze

Matthew 16:13–20
Built on a Strong Foundation

Lesson 26: No One Has a Higher Rank in God's Kingdom

Activities

Review Activity: **Humility Crossword Puzzle**
Memory Work: **Review the *Magnificat***
Coloring Page: **Stop Trying to Be In Charge!**

Review Activity

Humility Crossword Puzzle

Materials

- Pencil
- Humility Crossword Puzzle (Student Page 223)

Directions

1 Tear out Student Page 223, the Humility Crossword Puzzle.
2 Using the pencil, have the student fill in the blanks. If he can't remember an answer, read the relevant section from the lesson, as a hint. The answers are given in parentheses after each clue here, but not in the student's page.

Clues
DOWN
1 The followers or _________ of Jesus wanted to know who would be the greatest. (disciples)
2 Jesus said, "Whoever _________ himself like this little child is greatest." (humbles)
4 The kingdom that Jesus came to build is called the kingdom of _________. (heaven)
6 Jesus' disciples asked who would have the highest _________. (rank)

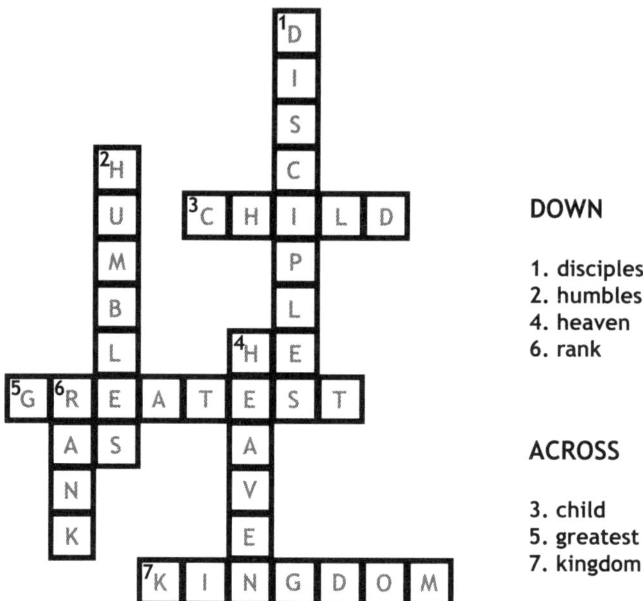

Memory Work

• •

Review the *Magnificat*

Materials

- The *Magnificat* (Student Page 225; can also be found in Luke 1:46–49)
- OPTIONAL: Crayons, markers, or colored pencils

Directions

1 Tear out Student Page 225, which contains the text of the memory verses.
2 Say to the student, "Let's review these verses we've been learning. Mary said this prayer-poem to God, and we can say it too."
3 Say, "Let's say the first line together two times: My soul glorifies the Lord, and my spirit rejoices in God my Savior." *[Say this line together two times.]*
4 Say, "Good! Now let's say the next line together: For he has been mindful of the humble state of his servant." *[Say this line together two times.]*
5 Continue to add a phrase at a time, through to the end of the verses.
6 Say, "Now let's try to say the whole prayer together . . ." *Help the student say the entire prayer, giving help and encouragement wherever necessary.*
7 (Optional) Have the student decorate the Student Page, to keep in his room this week and review.

220

Stop Trying to Be In Charge!

Jesus' twelve disciples wanted to be of higher ranks than other followers of Jesus. But he told them that in his kingdom, everyone is following God together.

Humility Crossword Puzzle

DOWN

1. The followers or ____________ of Jesus wanted to know who would be the greatest.

2. Jesus said, "Whoever __________ himself like this little child is greatest."

4. The kingdom that Jesus came to build is called the kingdom of __________ .

6. Jesus' disciples asked who would have the highest __________ .

ACROSS

3. When the disciples asked a question, Jesus answered by showing them a little __________ .

5. Jesus' disciples asked, "Who is the ______________ in the kingdom of heaven?"

7. In Jesus' ____________, no one is greater than other people.

The Magnificat: Luke 1:46–49

My soul glorifies the Lord,
and my spirit rejoices in God my
Savior, for he has been mindful of
the humble state of his servant.
From now on all generations will
call me blessed, for the Mighty
One has done great things for
me—holy is his name.

Matthew 18:1-4
Jesus Shows the Disciples What Being Humble Means

Lesson 27: Jesus Leaves No One Out

Activities

Service Activity: **Acts of Kindness in Jesus' Name**
Game: **Names of God Around the World**
Coloring Page: **In the King's Name**

Service Activity

Acts of Kindness in Jesus' Name

Materials

(will vary)

Directions

1   Say to the student, "Even small acts of kindness done in Jesus' name count—like giving someone a cool drink of water. Whatever you do for others in Jesus' name matters to Jesus—big things or small things."

2   Help the student find three acts of service of her own, or from the following list. As she completes these jobs or activities remind her to declare out loud, or silently in her mind, that she is doing them in the name of Jesus. Any act of service can be used.

- Get a thirsty person a drink (water, juice, tea, etc . . .)
- Serve (or even make) a meal for someone
- Help with another person's chore
- Clean up someone else's mess
- Play or read with a younger sibling
- Make a card or draw a picture for someone in a nursing home or a hospital
- Go through old toys/clothes/etc. and collect items to take to Goodwill or other thrift store
- [With parental supervision] Take a bag and clean up trash along the road in your neighborhood
- Taking the "helping with another person's chore" a step further, offer to help a parent, relative, neighbor, friend with a project (painting a room, cleaning a room or straightening up outside, moving boxes, decorating the house for a party or a holiday, collecting trash to take to the dump, etc.)

- Write out a prayer for someone (or a group) you care about (to give to them or to keep by the bedside to pray for them)
- Write down seven encouragements for members of your family or class. Share one from your list with one of your family members or classmates every day for one week.
- Offer your sibling your computer time/game time [or whatever type of special extra-curricular activity is a privilege in your house] for a day OR spend one of those times playing with a sibling rather than entertaining yourself

Game

Names of God Around the World

Materials

- Pen or pencil
- Names of God Around the World (Student Page 231)

Directions

1. Tear out Student Page 231, "Names of God Around the World."
2. Say to the student, "People where we live, in the United States, are not the only people who believe in God. There are people in other places who believe in God too! Many of them speak different languages. They all have different words that mean "God.""
3. Say each country, and pronounce their word for God (see list below). As you pronounce the word for God, have the student draw a line from the country to the correct word that you are saying. (If the student has trouble connecting the foreign word you're saying and the corresponding word written on the page, give help, to prevent this activity from becoming too frustrating.)
4. Answers (to be read out loud so child can draw lines): Latin—Deus *[say DAY-uss]*, Hebrew—Elohim *[say el-oh-HEEM]*, Italian—Dio *[say DEE-oh]*, German—Gott *[say GOTT]*, English—God, Irish—Dia, French—Dieu *[say dyUH]*, Danish—Gut *[say GOOT]*, Polish—Bog, Russian—Bojh, Greek—Theos, Swahili—Mungu *[say MOON-goo]*

Coloring Page

In the King's Name

In this lesson Jesus told the disciples about other people who were also doing things "in Jesus' name." Think of a king who sends out one of his messengers to a distant part of the kingdom to deliver a message. The messenger arrives at the castle and knocks on the wooden gates and says "Open up *in the name of the king.*" That means the people need to open up the door as if the king himself were knocking. The person Jesus is talking about in this story is like this messenger. Even though he is not one of the twelve disciples, he is following King Jesus and doing his bidding, just like the disciples are.

Names of God Around the World

Language	Name for God
Swahili	Bog
Latin	Theos
Hebrew	Mungu
Italian	Bojh
German	Dio
English	Gut
Irish	God
French	Dieu
Danish	Gott
Polish	Dia
Russian	Elohim
Greek	Deus

Mark 9:38–41
I Have Come in the Name of the King!

Lesson 28: Jesus' Followers Are Servants, Not Commanders

Activities

Put It Into Practice Activity: **Put Others First**
Group Game: **Two Kinds of Leaders**
Memory Work: **The Lord's Prayer, Part I**
Coloring Page: **A Different Kind of Kingdom**

Put It Into Practice Activity (Individual or Group)

Put Others First

Children love to "be first" and "go first" and "have it first." In this lesson there is a strong emphasis on not serving ourselves first, and this is a good opportunity for your student to put this into practice. This could also be done with multiple students.

Materials

- Putting Others First Chart (Student Page 239)
- Stickers
- Pen or Marker
- Some kind of reward for the student to receive if he reaches the goal

Directions

1. Tear out Student Page 239, with the Putting Others First Chart.
2. Tell the student, "In this week's lesson, Jesus told us to put others first. Sometimes that's not easy, because we want to be first all the time. So this week we're going to practice this."
3. Show the student the chart, and say, "Each time that you put someone else first, we'll put a sticker on that day's spot on the chart, and we'll write down what you did. If you fill up the whole row with stickers by the end of the week, you will get a reward!"
4. Help the child think of some examples of putting others first. Here are a few suggestions:
   - Let a sibling use the bathroom first
   - Serve someone else a drink before getting your own

     – Let someone else play with a toy before you do

     – Volunteer to set the table (or some other common household chore) before being asked

5   Throughout the week, observe the student. Notice (and praise) any instances of putting others first. Record these instances on the chart by placing a sticker in the appropriate spot and writing down what the action was.

6   Be sure to remind the student, each day, of this activity, so that he doesn't forget during the week.

7   If the student reaches the goal by the end of the week, give him the reward. (Even if he doesn't get all the way to the end of the chart, if there has been significant effort, go ahead and reward him anyway).

8   Tell the student, "Jesus said that he came to serve people, not to boss them around. He wants us to be the same way." Encourage the student to begin building these acts of service into habits.

Group Game

· ·

Two Kinds of Leaders

Directions

1   Tell the students, "In this week's lesson, James and John thought that they knew how to be leaders. So they wanted to hurry up and get positions of power and authority. <u>But they really just wanted to tell people what to do</u>. Today we'll play a game where we have two different kinds of leaders, and you'll see how a good leader behaves."

2   Have all the students spread out in the center of the room and face the front of the room. Select one student to be a "Student Leader." Tell the students, "in this game you will be following two leaders." Have this student stand at the front of the room, while the teacher stands at the opposite end, both facing the students who are spread out in the center, like this:

Student Leader

Student   Student   Student

Student   Student   Student

Student   Student   Student   Student

Teacher

Make sure that all students are facing the Student Leader and are arm's length apart so they don't collide with each other during the various poses that they will be doing.

3   Tell the students that everyone will be spelling out words with their arms and legs one letter at a time. No student, except for the Student Leader up front, should look back at the teacher.

4   Explain to the students that you will be speaking directions to them, and that they should follow those directions to pose in ways that you tell them. These poses will form letters. You, the teacher, will be performing that same action behind them, but they

shouldn't look back to see what you're doing. Every student except the Student Leader at the front of the room should attempt to follow your directions. After the students have tried to do what you told them, ask the Student Leader (who has been able to see your action from his vantage point) to repeat the directions again and imitate the action you've just done. Ask the students if they know which letter they have created with their shape. Make sure that everyone knows which letter was performed before moving on to the next letter in the word. Remind the students that your directions will pose them into the shapes of letters that spell out a word. <u>The first student to guess the word, wins.</u> *[The word, which you should not reveal to the students yet, is "SERVANT."]*

5 *Note to teacher: Your verbal directions will be intentionally vague, and shouldn't include many details, because you are being an example of a "bad leader" who tells people what to do without demonstrating it.*

6 First Letter: say and act out the first direction: "Crouch down, with your knees bent, and bend your arms out in front of you." *[The letter is S.]*

7 With the students still looking straight ahead, tell the Student Leader to imitate what you are doing. He will pose in the same way that you have just done.

8 See if the students can guess what letter the Student Leader is forming. If no one can guess, you may tell them.

9 Second Letter: say and act out the second direction: "Face the right wall. Hold both hands out, one above the other, and stick your leg out toward that wall too." *[The letter is E.]*

10 Third Letter: say and act out the third direction: "Face the front wall. Make an O with your arm, and hold leg out at an angle." *[The letter is R.]*

11 Fourth Letter: "Sit on the floor. Hold one leg and one arm up in the air." *[The letter is V.]*

12 Fifth Letter: "Stand up, with your legs wide apart. Then stick your elbows out and fold your hands in front of your chest." *[The letter is A.]*

13 Sixth Letter: Bend over and touch the floor with your hands, making a rainbow shape out of your body. *[The letter is n (lowercase N).]*

14 Seventh Letter: "Stand up straight, let your head hang down, and hold both arms straight out to the sides." *[The letter is T.]*

15 If a student guesses which word is being spelled, he or she becomes the new Student Leader. You can then use this method to spell other words, such as "Leader" or "Jesus" or "God."

16 At the end of the game after the students have spelled out a few words, ask the students in the center of the room "Which leader was easier to follow—the one who just ordered you around, or the one who showed you what to do? Which leader would you rather follow? James and John wanted to order people what to do, but Jesus doesn't just tell people what to do; he does it too."

Memory Work

The Lord's Prayer, Part I

Materials

- The Lord's Prayer, Part I (Student Page 241)
- (Optional) crayons, markers, or colored pencils to decorate the page

Directions

1 Tear out Student Page 241, containing "The Lord's Prayer, Part I."

2 Tell the student, "Jesus gave his disciples a way to pray, to help them talk to God. It is sometimes called 'The Lord's Prayer.' We can talk to God in our own words; we don't have to use these exact words. But these tell us some things that we should be praying for—things that Jesus says are important to pray for. This week we're going to learn part of the Lord's Prayer."

3 Say, "I'll say the first line of the prayer, and then we'll say it together two times: Our Father in heaven." *[Say together twice: Our Father in heaven.]*

4 Say, "The next line of the prayer asks that we and everybody else would respect and worship God as much as he deserves. It says 'Hallowed be your name.' Let's say that together twice." *[Say together twice: Hallowed be your name.]*

5 Say, "Now let's put those two lines together, and say them twice: Our Father in heaven, hallowed be your name." *[Say together twice: Our Father in heaven, hallowed be your name.]*

6 Say, "The next line of the prayer asks that God's kingdom would come and that God's will would be done. Do you remember how in the lessons this year, Jesus has been talking a lot about the kingdom of God? That is when everything will be the way it's supposed to be, with people loving God and each other. We want that to happen, so we pray for it. We also see it starting now, whenever we show other people the same kindness that God shows to us. Say these lines twice after me: Your kingdom come, your will be done on earth as it is in heaven." *[Say together twice: Your kingdom come, your will be done on earth as it is in heaven.]*

7 Say, "We've gotten halfway through the Lord's Prayer. Let's say together what we've learned so far." *[Say the following together with the student, giving any needed help: Our Father in heaven, hallowed be your name. Your kingdom come, your will be done on earth as it is in heaven.]*

8 (Optional step) Let the student decorate the Lord's Prayer page, using the crayons or markers or colored pencils.

9 Over the next few days, review the prayer at least once a day with the student, using the Student Page as a prompt.

Coloring Page

· ·

A Different Kind of Kingdom

Two of the disciples, James and John, asked Jesus if they could be in charge of everybody else, if Jesus became king. The other disciples were jealous and got angry with James and John. They all wanted to be in charge. Instead, Jesus says that his followers must become servants. That means thinking first of how we can help others, instead of ourselves.

Putting Others First Chart

DAY 1	DAY 2	DAY 3	DAY 4	DAY 5	DAY 6	DAY 7

The Lord's Prayer, Part I

Our Father in heaven,

hallowed be your name,

your kingdom come,

your will be done,

on earth as it is in heaven.

Mark 10:35–45
Jesus Tells the Disciples Not to Fight About Who is the Greatest

243

Unit 7
Opposition to Jesus

Lesson 29: Jesus Upsets a Synagogue Service

Activities

Craft Project: **Make an Ancient Scroll**
Review Activity: **"Jesus in His Hometown" Word Search**
Memory Work: **Review the Lord's Prayer, Part I**
Coloring Page: **Jesus' Hometown is Angry with Him**

Craft Project

. . . .

Make an Ancient Scroll

Materials

- Scroll with Isaiah text, from Student Page 249
- ½ cup of instant coffee
- 1 cup of boiling water
- Coffee mug, large
- Spoon
- 9"x13" casserole dish
- Paper towels
- Aluminum foil (12" x 10")
- Two 10" long dowels (⅓" diameter), or two sticks of similar dimensions (smooth sticks will be easier to use than rough sticks)
- Liquid craft glue
- 6 spring-loaded clothespins
- OPTIONAL: three yards of brown yarn
- OPTIONAL: small rubber band (the size that comes around bunches of asparagus)

Directions

1　Preheat oven to 200 degrees. Remove Student Page 249 from the book along the perforation lines. Have the student help you crumple the page up, and then flatten it again.
2　In the coffee mug, help the student stir instant coffee into the boiling water. Pour this mixture into the casserole dish.

3   Lay out a double thickness of paper towels to be ready for the wet paper. Submerge Student Page 249 in the casserole dish of coffee. Leave it there for 5–10 minutes; the longer you leave it in, the darker it will get. When desired, have the student remove the page from the coffee, and carefully place on the paper towels to drain.

4   Cut off a piece of aluminum foil that is larger than the page. Carefully transfer the damp page from the paper towel to the foil. Place the foil in the preheated oven.

5   After seven minutes, remove the page and foil from the oven. Peel the dried page off of the foil. To create an even more "aged" appearance, very gently crumple and recrumple it.

6   Squeeze a line of glue across the left edge of the page (be generous!). Lay the dowel or stick down on the glue, and roll it, with the paper, one revolution (see illustration). Secure the paper (glue inside), with five clothespins. Repeat along the right edge of the page. Allow to dry. If you want to create simulated "stains," have the student use her fingers to sprinkle a few drops of water onto the page. When the drops dry, they will look like stains from years of use.

7   Once the scroll is completely dry, use the sticks to roll each end of your scroll up, until the ends meet in the middle.

OPTIONAL:

If desired, make a tie for your scroll. Tie one end of a three-yard piece of brown yarn to a rubber band (the size that comes on bunches of asparagus). Roll the rest of the yarn into a ball, and then wrap the yarn around the rubber band by passing the ball through the rubber band over and over and over and over. Once you have covered the rubber band with the yarn, tie the two ends together tightly.

Review Activity

"Jesus in His Hometown" Word Search

Materials

- "Jesus in His Hometown" Word Search (Student Page 251)
- Pencil

Directions

1   Tear out Student Page 251.
2   Say to the student, "Look for the words from this week's lesson that are hidden in the word search. Some run left to right; some run top to bottom. One is written diagonally."
3   If needed, help the student find the words.

    - Angry
    - Anointed
    - Blind
    - Cliff
    - Crowd
    - Galilee
    - Jesus
    - Leprosy

- Nazareth
- Prisoners
- Prophet
- Reading
- Scripture
- Scroll
- Spirit

4 Use the answer key below to help you if needed:

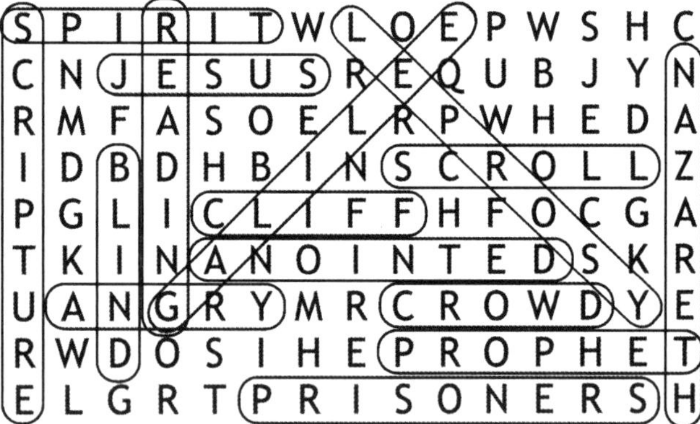

Memory Work

• •

Review the Lord's Prayer, Part I

Materials

- The Lord's Prayer, Part I (Student Page 241 from Lesson 28)

Directions

Say to the student, "Remember, in the last lesson we learned the first part of a prayer Jesus taught his disciples to pray. It was called the Lord's Prayer. Let's say that first half together, twice."

[Together, twice]: Our Father in heaven, hallowed be your name. Your kingdom come, your will be done on earth as it is in heaven.

Coloring Page

• •

Jesus' Hometown is Angry with Him

Jesus told the people that he was the one who had been predicted by the ancient prophecies. He said that they would reject him, just as many of their ancestors had rejected the old prophets. When he said that they wouldn't understand him, the people became angry and wanted to kill him!

The Spirit of the Lord is on me, because
he has anointed me to preach
good news to the poor.
He has sent me to
proclaim freedom for the prisoners and
recovery of sight for the blind,
to release the oppressed,
to proclaim the year
of the Lord's favor.

Isaiah 61: 1-2

```
S P I R I T W L O E P W S H C
C N J E S U S R E Q U B J Y N
R M F A S O E L R P W H E D A
I D B D H B I N S C R O L L Z
P G L I C L I F F H F O C G A
T K I N A N O I N T E D S K R
U A N G R Y M R C R O W D Y E
R W D O S I H E P R O P H E T
E I G R T P R I S O N E R S H
```

Luke 4:14–30
An Angry Crowd Chases Jesus Out of Town

Lesson 30: False Teaching Spreads Like Yeast

Activities

Group Game: **Following the Right Directions**
Cooking/Science Activity: **The Silent, Spreading Effect of Yeast**
Activity: **Bread Maze**
Memory Work: **The Lord's Prayer, Part II**
Coloring Page: **But That's Not True!**

Group Game

Following the Right Directions

In this week's lesson, Jesus warned against false teachers who will say untrue things about God. This group game reminds us to follow the right directions.

Materials

- Blindfold
- Chair for every student except three

Directions

1 Select one student to be blindfolded, and take him to one end or one corner of the room. Tie the blindfold around his eyes and make sure he cannot see through, under, or over it.

2 Have the other students place their chairs randomly in the center of the room, creating obstacles between the blindfolded student and the path to the other side. Have the non-blindfolded students sit in the chairs, except for two of them who will be direction-givers (see steps 3 and 4).

3 Tell the blindfolded student, "Two students will stand behind you on either side and give you directions. One of the students will give correct directions, and the other will give fake directions. You will need to decide which student to listen to. If you run into an obstacle, both students giving directions will switch places with the two closest 'obstacles' and you will continue from there with two new students to give directions."

4 Quietly, out of earshot of the blindfolded student, select one of the two direction-givers to give true directions around the obstacles, and tell the other one to make up false directions—to say anything that is the opposite of what the blindfolded student should actually do.

5   Tell the seated students, "Once _______ *[blindfolded student's name]* and the two direction-givers start walking toward the goal, I want you to start calling out false instructions, like 'Back up three steps!' or 'Turn left now!' or 'You went too far.' Try to fool him!" Encourage them to be loud in their false-direction-giving. The seated students may also chose to hold their arms out in the path, but they must not move their arms around.

6   Gently spin the blindfolded student around a couple of times (just enough to disorient him slightly) and then, gently, point him in the direction of his goal and tell him to begin walking slowly. Walk in front of him, backwards, not touching him. Stay close enough to catch him if he seems about to trip or to tumble over a classmate's chair.

7   When the student reaches the goal, quiet the rest of the students, and praise him for following the correct directions. Ask if it was hard to hear the true directions with all the false ones being called out. Say, "In this week's lesson we learned to be careful not to pay attention to untrue things that people say about God. Those untrue directions will lead us into trouble, just like the fake directions in this game would keep you from reaching your goal."

8   Pick a different student to walk the path. You may want to rearrange the chairs before this second round, to keep it challenging.

Cooking/Science Activity

The Silent, Spreading Effect of Yeast (an Overnight No-Knead Bread Recipe)

Materials

- 6 cups white flour, divided, plus extra for flouring a work surface and sprinkling on the bread loaf
- 3 Tbsp lukewarm water, divided, plus 2 Tbsp water, divided
- ¼ tsp active dry yeast, divided
- 3 tsp salt, divided
- Sharp knife
- Baking sheet
- Kitchen towels
- Cornmeal for baking (a handful; enough to sprinkle generously on the baking sheet)

Directions

Note: This project is done over the course of two days. It works well to do the first part in the mid-afternoon of the first day, around 4 pm, so that the second part can be done during the morning of the next day.

1   In a large mixing bowl, have the student help you stir together 3 cups of the flour, 1½ cups of the lukewarm water, and 1½ tsp of the salt. Mix it well, but don't try to use your hands, as it will be very sticky.

2 Say to the student, "Now we are going to mix together another bowl of the same ingredients, but this time we will add a very small amount of yeast. Remember from this week's lesson that yeast mixes with the dough and gives off carbon dioxide gas, which makes air bubbles in the bread dough. After we mix it, we will wait to see the difference between the bowl with yeast and the bowl without it."

3 In a second large mixing bowl, have the student help you stir together 3 cups flour, 1½ cups lukewarm water, 1½ tsp salt, and ¼ tsp yeast. <u>Point out what a small amount of yeast you are mixing in, compared with the large quantities of flour and water.</u> Mix well. Cover both bowls with kitchen towels, and leave at room temperature until the next morning around 8 am.

4 The next morning, let the student uncover the bowls. The dough in the bowl with yeast will have doubled in size and developed many bubbles. The other bowl should look exactly the same. Talk with the student about how those tiny, few grains of yeast worked their way all through the dough, and changed it tremendously.

5 To actually make bread out of your risen dough, first sprinkle flour to cover your work surface. Scrape the risen dough onto this surface, and then, with well-floured hands, shape the dough into a loaf by folding the corners to the center, forming a seam. On a large baking sheet, have the student shake a generous amount of cornmeal. Place the loaf on the baking sheet, with the seam on the bottom.

6 Shake flour over a clean kitchen towel, and place this over the loaf. Set in a warm place, and allow to rise for 90 minutes. Preheat your oven to 425 degrees F so that it will be ready at the end of this rise. When the 90 minutes are over, remove the towel, slash the top of the loaf with a sharp, wet knife, and place the baking sheet on the middle rack of your oven. Bake for 55 minutes, or until the loaf sounds hollow when tapped on the bottom. Allow to cool, and enjoy!

7 If you desire, you can "bake" the contents of the other bowl in order to compare the difference and observe the effect of the yeast.

Activity

· ·

Bread Maze

Materials

- Pencil
- Bread Maze (Student Page 261)

Directions

1 Tear out the Bread Maze, Student Page 261.
2 Say to the student, "In this week's lesson, Jesus used bread as a way to talk to his disciples about people who were teaching untrue things. Avoiding these untrue teachings can sometimes be difficult, but it is important."
3 Have the student solve the maze with his pencil. Tell him to make sure to avoid the Pharisees in the middle of the maze.

· ·

The Lord's Prayer, Part II

Materials

- The Lord's Prayer, Part II (Student Page 263)
- (Optional) crayons, colored pencils, or markers to decorate the page

Directions

1 Tear out Student Page 263, The Lord's Prayer, Part II, and refer to it as you teach the prayer to the child in the following steps.

2 Say to the student, "We have learned the first half of the prayer that Jesus taught his disciples—the Lord's Prayer. Let's say that first half together." *[Say together: Our Father in heaven, hallowed be your name. Your kingdom come, your will be done on earth as it is in heaven.]*

3 Say, "Today we will learn the rest of the prayer. The next thing it tells us to ask God is "Give us today our daily bread." This means 'God, please give us food and everything we need for today.' God is the one who takes care of us and gives us what we need. Let's say that line twice together: Give us today our daily bread." *[Say twice, together: Give us today our daily bread.]*

4 Say, "The next line asks God to forgive us our debts, and says that we will forgive other people too. We don't owe God a 'debt' of money; this is talking about bad things we've done, that we're asking God to forgive. Do you remember back in Lesson 4, when Jesus said we are like a servant who owed his king a bazillion dollars, and the king forgave it? That's how God is with us. When we ask him to forgive us, he does. And he helps us forgive other people too. So let's say that line together twice now: And forgive us our debts, as we also have forgiven our debtors." *[Say together, twice, giving any necessary help: And forgive us our debts, as we also have forgiven our debtors.]*

5 So let's combine the two lines we've learned today. Say these after me: Give us today our daily bread, and forgive us our debts, as we also have forgiven our debtors."

6 Now we'll learn the last part of the prayer, where we pray for God's protection. We're not very good at doing the right thing; we need God's help every day. So we pray, 'And lead us not into temptation, but deliver us from evil.' Say that line with me twice now." *[Say together, twice: And lead us not into temptation, but deliver us from evil.]*

7 Say, "Good! Now let's put together the second half of the prayer, the part we learned today. I'll say it with you." *[Say together: Give us today our daily bread, and forgive us our debts, as we also have forgiven our debtors. And lead us not into temptation, but deliver us from evil.]*

8 Say, "Now let's put the whole prayer together. Say it with me. *[Say together, helping whenever necessary, since this is a large amount of text to memorize: Our Father in heaven, hallowed be your name. Your kingdom come, your will be done, on earth as it is in heaven. Give us today our daily bread, and forgive us our debts, as we also have forgiven our debtors. And lead us not into temptation, but deliver us from evil.]*

9 (Optional step) Let the student decorate the Lord's Prayer page, using the crayons or markers or colored pencils.

10 The student probably won't have the prayer perfectly memorized right away, but encourage him, and pray the prayer with him over the coming days. Help him to think of this as a real prayer to God, and not just a set of memorized lines. If possible, help him think of specific applications of the phrases of the prayer [what "daily bread" is he praying for or giving thanks for? What temptation or hard situation might he ask God's help with? Etc.]. Keep the decorated Student Page copy of the prayer in a prominent place, such as in his room or on the refrigerator, to remind you both to pray the prayer.

Coloring Page

But That's Not True!

In this week's lesson, we heard about people who were teaching untrue things about God. This picture shows a classroom where a teacher has just said something untrue about history. She said that Abraham Lincoln was the first president of the United States of America (do you see President Lincoln's picture on the wall of the classroom)? But one student is raising her hand to speak, because she knows the truth: Lincoln was not the first president. Knowing the truth helps us to see when people are saying things that aren't true.

Bread Maze

Watch out for the Pharisees!

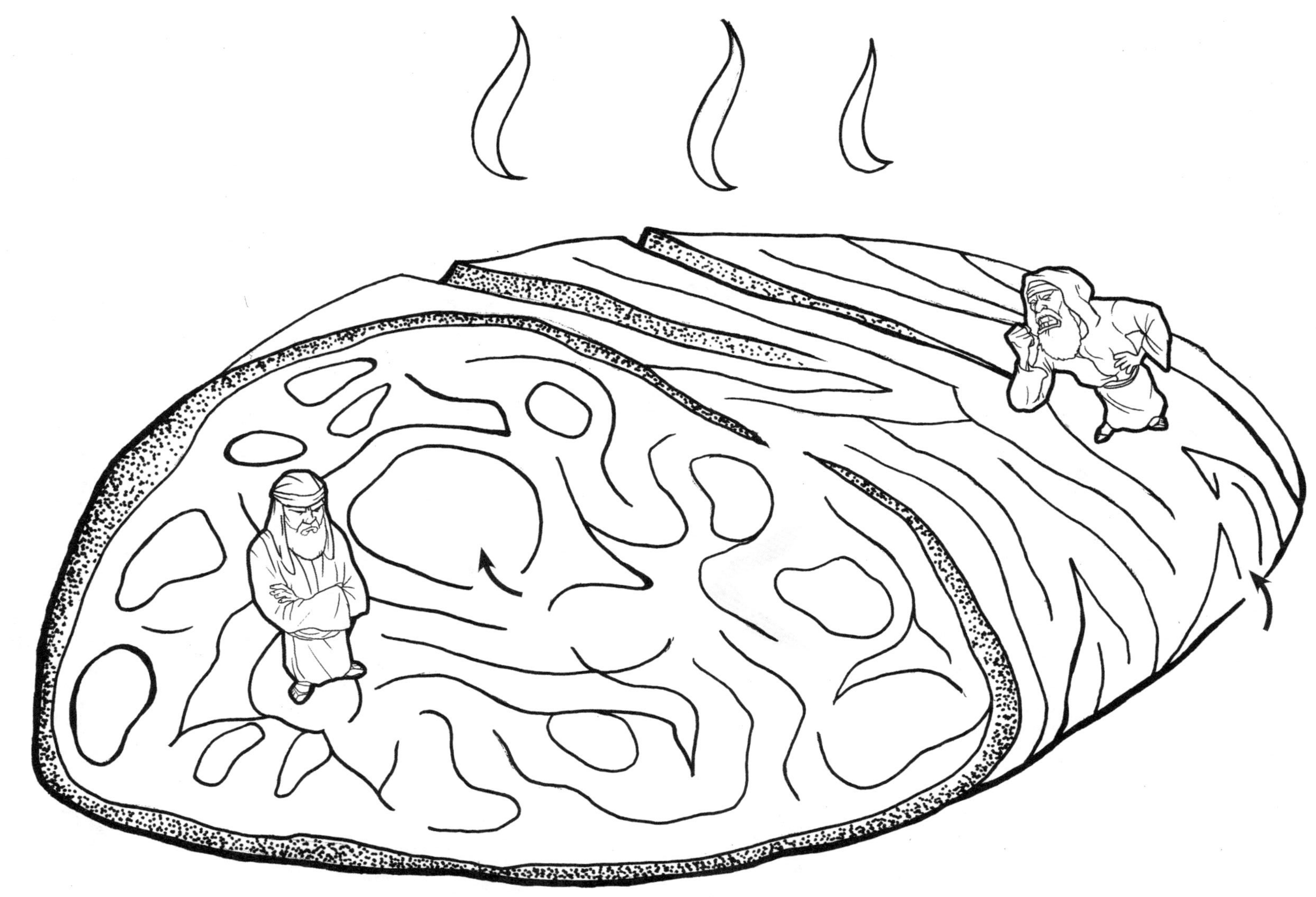

The Lord's Prayer, Part II

Our Father in heaven,

hallowed be your name,

your kingdom come,

your will be done,

on earth as it is in heaven.

Give us today our daily bread.

And forgive us our debts,

as we also have forgiven our debtors.

And lead us not into temptation,

but deliver us from evil.

Matthew 16:5–12
But That's Not True!

Lesson 31: A Clean Heart is Better Than Clean Food

Activities

Review/Game: **What Makes Us Unclean on the Inside?**
Science Activity: **Getting Really Clean**
Craft Project: **Find the Secret of Being Clean**
Memory Work: **Review the Lord's Prayer, Part II**
Coloring Page: **Rules on Top of Rules**

Review Game

. . . .

What Makes Us Unclean On The Inside?

Materials

- Quart-sized mason jar
- Person-shaped wrapper, from Student Activity Page 271
- Tape
- Crayons, colored pencils, or markers
- Student Activity Page 273 (chart of foods, actions, and attitudes)
- Scissors
- OPTIONAL: Timer

Directions

1 Have the student color and cut out the person-shaped wrapper. Together, tape it around the outside of the mason jar.
2 Have the student cut along the lines on Student Activity Page 273 (the chart). Fold each slip of paper, and put it into the mason jar.
3 Instruct the student to pull one slip of paper out at a time. Have her read the item on the paper, and then decide whether it makes the mason jar person clean, unclean, or doesn't matter. If she has trouble remembering, remind her of what Jesus said in today's lesson (see *Instructor Text*, pages 110 and 111)

4   As she goes through the slips, make piles for "clean," "unclean," and "doesn't matter." At the end of the game, all foods should be in the "doesn't matter" pile, the positive actions and attitudes should be in the "clean" pile, and the negative actions and attitudes should be in the "unclean" pile.

5   To ramp up the excitement, set a timer for your student, and see how fast she can do it!

Science Activity

Getting Really Clean

Materials

- Vegetable oil
- Ground cinnamon
- Hand soap
- Running water

Directions

1   Pour a quarter-sized circle of oil into the student's hand. Then give a good sprinkle of cinnamon over it. Instruct the student to rub the oil and cinnamon all over her hands.
2   Have the student try to wash the cinnamon off with cold water. See what happens.
3   Have the student try to wash the cinnamon off with warm water. Is this more effective?
4   Have the student try the cinnamon off with warm water and soap. How long does it take to really get all the cinnamon off?
5   Talk with the student about how we often think that a quick rinse under cold water is enough to clean our hands—but actually soap, warm water, and a lengthy rinsing are necessary. This experiment used cinnamon, which is harmless, because it's easy to see; but germs are invisible, and harmful, so it is much more important to wash properly.
6   Say to the student, "The Pharisees thought that they were making people get really clean, but they weren't cleaning the things that were important."

Craft Project

Find the Secret of Being Clean

Materials

- The Secret of Being Clean (Student Page 275)
- Crayons or Markers (three different colors: we suggest blue, green, and red, but any three will work)

Directions

1   Tear out Student Page 275.

2 Say to the student, "In this week's lesson, we learned that being 'clean' is about more than just washing your hands. Jesus told us the secret of where real cleanness comes from. Color the spaces in this picture to reveal what that secret is."

3 Have the student use her three crayons or markers to color the numbers. Make sure that she uses one color for all the "1" spaces, a different one for all the "2" spaces, and a third color for all the "3" spaces. We suggest blue for 1, green for 2, and red for 3.

4 When the spaces are all colored, a picture of a heart should be revealed in the palm of the hand. Point to the heart and say to the student: "What is that?" When she answers that it is a heart, say: "That is the answer to the question on this page: A clean **heart** is more important than clean hands."

Memory Work

· ·

Review the Lord's Prayer, Part II

Materials

- The Lord's Prayer, Part II (Student Page 263 from Lesson 30, if you still have it)

Directions

Say to the student, "Last week you learned the Lord's Prayer. Let's review it to make sure it stays in your memory. The first half said, 'Our Father in heaven, hallowed be your name. Your kingdom come, your will be done on earth as it is in heaven.' Let's say that part together."
[Say together: Our Father in heaven, hallowed be your name. Your kingdom come, your will be done on earth as it is in heaven.]
Say, "Then the second half said, 'Give us today our daily bread, and forgive us our debts, as we also have forgiven our debtors. And lead us not into temptation, but deliver us from evil.' Let's say that part together." *[Say together: Give us today our daily bread, and forgive us our debts, as we also have forgiven our debtors. And lead us not into temptation, but deliver us from evil.]*
If the student has a good grasp on the first and second halves of the prayer, say the whole thing together.

Coloring Page

· ·

Rules on Top of Rules

God had given the Jewish people special rules about their food, but over time, some of the leaders and teachers had added extra rules. It would be like if your mother said, "Don't eat the cake that is in the refrigerator," and then your older brother decided that you shouldn't even **open** the refrigerator, just to make sure you didn't eat any cake. That would be more rules than your mother wanted you to have.

Mason Jar Wrapper

Clean and Unclean Chart

pizza	apple slices	feeling jealous of your sister
fish sticks	ice cream	milk
lying	cleaning up a mess without being asked	bread
having a cheerful attitude	carrots	interrupting someone who is speaking
orange juice	saying mean, angry things to your friend	chicken
sharing	obeying your parents right away	macaroni

The Secret of Being Clean

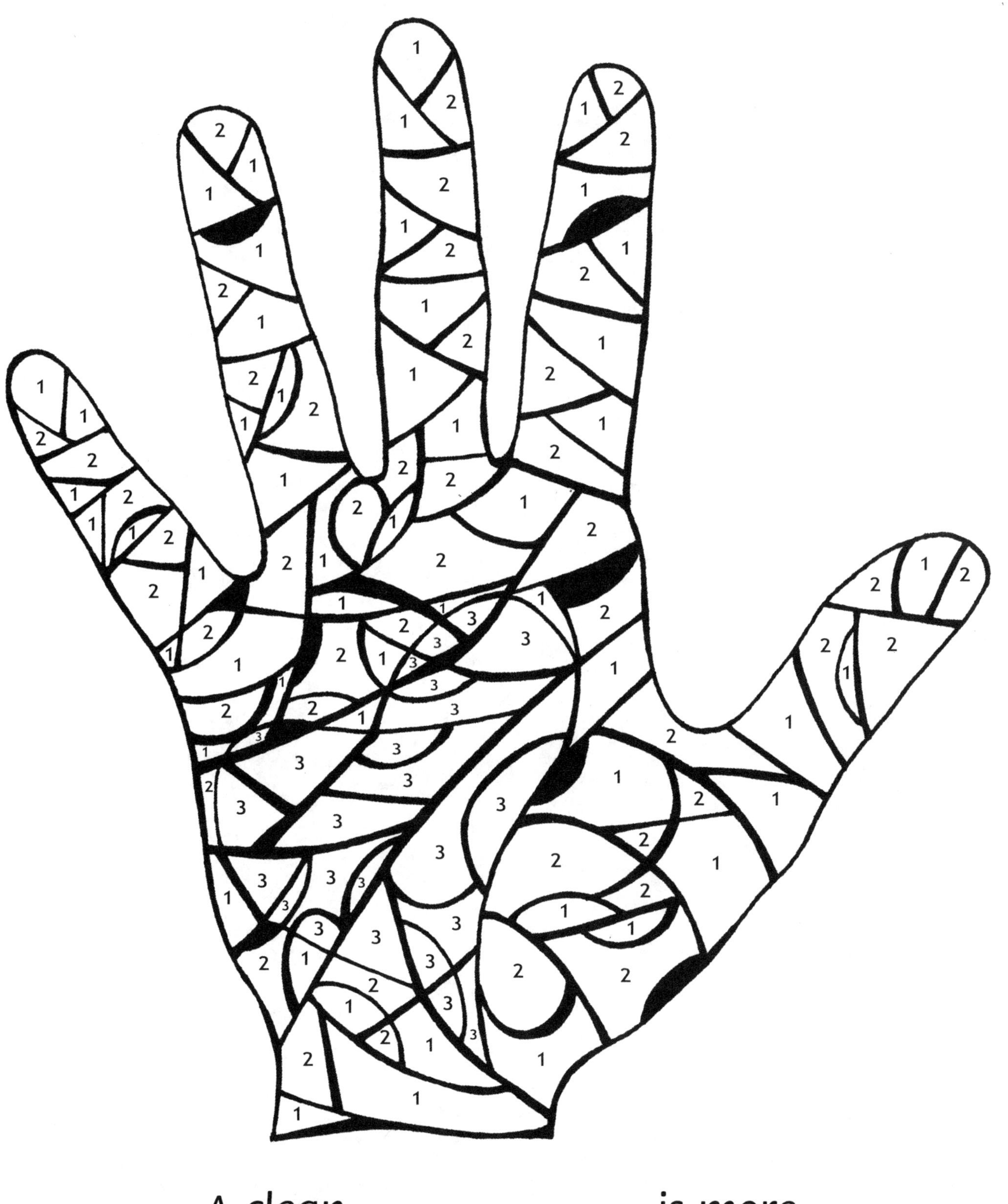

A clean _______________ is more
important than clean hands.

Matthew 15:1–20
Rules on Top of Rules

Lesson 32: Surrendering Our Lives to God Every Day

Activities

Craft Project: **Make a Wooden Cross**
Memory Work: **Review the Lord's Prayer**
Coloring Page: **Peter Tries to Stop Jesus**

Craft Project

· ·

Make a Wooden Cross

Materials
- 2 pieces of 2x4 wood (one 11 inches long and the other 8 inches long)
- 2 nails
- Hammer
- (optional) Paint and brush
- Push pins
- Piece of strong fishing-line or wire
- Small pieces of paper (about 2x3 inches in size)
- Pen

Directions

1   Hammer the two pieces of wood together in the shape of a cross. Have your child paint it if desired. Let it dry.
2   Nail the piece of string onto the back of the cross in a loop shape for hanging. On the pieces of paper, have the student write ways he can "take up his cross" and "lose his life" by serving God instead of serving himself. If handwriting this much content is a struggle for your student, have him dictate some ideas to you, and you can write them out.
    Some suggestions:

    – Clean up a mess that is not your own (serving others)
    – Let your sibling sit in the spot that you want to sit in (selflessness)
    – Let a friend play with something that is very special to you (sharing)
    – Walk away from a fight (peacefulness)
    – Talk about something calmly instead of yelling or throwing a tantrum (self-control)

     – Instead of waking up grumpy about doing your chores or school work, choose to have a good attitude (joyfulness)
     – Offer to read Scripture aloud with your family or say a prayer out loud (faithfulness)
     – Spend time reading or playing with a younger sibling or a younger friend (love)
     – Offer to help your parents in the kitchen or with outside chores (kindness)

3 Fold up the pieces of paper and pin them into the cross. Hang the cross on your child's wall. As the student tries to put these things into practice, talk with him about what the lesson said: we are to serve God and others, more than we try to get what *we* want. This is hard, but Jesus helps us to live this way.

Memory Work

The Lord's Prayer

Remember to review the Lord's Prayer this week.

Coloring Page

Peter Tries to Stop Jesus

Jesus told his disciples that he was going to Jerusalem, even though people would kill him when he got there. Peter didn't want to let that happen to Jesus, but Jesus told him it had to happen. Jesus was going to die for all of us because he loved us so much.

Matthew 16:21-26
Peter Tries to Stop Jesus from Going to Jerusalem

Unit 8

The End of Jesus' Life

Lesson 33: Obey God More Than Caesar

Activities

Craft Project: **Make a Personalized Denarius**
Group Game: **Caesar Says**
Coloring Page: **Caesar's Coins**

Craft Project

· ·

Make a Personalized Denarius

Materials

- Bowl
- Piece of stiff cardboard, at least 3 inches wide
- Black permanent marker
- Scissors or X-acto Knife
- Aluminum foil

Directions

1   Using the bowl as a circle-pattern, help the student trace a circle in the piece of cardboard and cut it out. Wrap the cardboard circle in aluminum foil so that it looks like a silver coin.

2   Tell the student, "A denarius was a little silver coin used in ancient Rome that had the face of the emperor on it. Now, we are going to pretend that you are the emperor of Rome. Then the coins in Rome would have *your* face on them. What would they look like then?"

3   Have the student draw a self-portrait on one face of the "coin" with the permanent marker. On the other side of the coin, have her write "This coin belongs to Emperor [*Student's Name*]."

4   Tell the student, "This coin is yours, because you made it and it has your face on it. It looks like you. You belong to God because he made you. God made you to be like him, just like you made this coin to be like you."

Group Game

Caesar Says

Directions

1   Have the students stand in a group. Select one student to be Caesar. Tell the students, "Today you are all members of the Roman Empire, and Caesar is your king. When he says to do something, you have to do it. But Jesus is even more powerful and important than Caesar. So when Jesus says something, everybody, even Caesar, has to obey."

2   Have the game go like a game of "Simon Says," except the Caesar student has to say "Caesar says," in order for a command to be valid. So, the student who is Caesar will say, "Caesar says touch your elbow," and everyone touches their elbow. But if she just says "Touch your elbow," without saying "Caesar says," then whoever performs the action is out.

3   At a few random moments, you, the instructor, should step in and say "Jesus says to . . . (stand on one leg, kneel down and pray, say something nice to the person next to you, etc)" When this happens, all of the students (including Caesar!) have to obey the command.

4   At the end of the game, remind everyone: "Jesus is greater than Caesar. Caesar ruled the whole Roman Empire, hundreds of thousands of people, but Jesus is the king of all people everywhere, even Caesar. We should do what Jesus says because he loves us and wants us to be happy."

Coloring Page

Caesar's Coins

In today's lesson, Jesus told people to give Caesar the coins he asked for. Caesar is important but God is more important. This is a picture of real coins from the time of Jesus. They have a picture of Caesar Tiberius on one side, and a picture of the emperor's mother Livia on the other.

Matthew 22:15–22
Obey God More than Caesar

Lesson 34: Jesus Introduces a New Exodus

Activities

Craft Project: **Make a Last Supper "Stained Glass" Page**
Cooking Activity: **Make Unleavened Bread**
Memory Work: **John 3:16**
Coloring Page: **The Last Supper**

Craft Project

. . . .

Make a Last Supper "Stained Glass" Page

Materials

- Picture of the elements from the Last Supper (Student Page 295)
- Bottle of white glue (note: after being used in this activity, this glue will no longer be white)
- Black acrylic paint
- Tablespoon measure
- Watercolor paints and brush
- Cup of water (to wash off and change colors)
- Paper towel sheet (to dry off your brush when you change colors)
- Hole punch
- String, yarn, or twine (enough to hang the picture in front of a window)

Directions

1 Measure out 1–2 tablespoons of black acrylic paint.
2 Add the 1–2 tablespoons of black paint to the bottle of white glue. Close the top and shake the bottle to mix the glue and paint, so that you end up with a bottle of black glue.
3 Tear out Student Page 295. Show it to the student and say, "Here is a picture of grapes, a cup, and bread. This is to remind us of the bread and the wine from the special meal that Jesus ate with his disciples. We're going to decorate this picture."
4 Have the student squeeze the black glue along the thick black lines of the objects in the picture. Allow the glue to dry. This will leave a raised black outline of the coloring page.

5   Once the glue is completely dried, have the student use the watercolors and brush to
    lightly paint in the rest of the image between the raised outlines. Have the student use
    the cup of water and paper towel sheet to clean off and dry the brush every time he
    wants to change colors. He may also use the black glue to make a thicker black border
    around the paper and then use watercolors to paint in the background as well.

6   To get an "illuminated" effect, help the student punch a hole in the top of the picture and
    thread string or yarn through it to hang the picture in front of a window that receives lots
    of light.

Cooking Activity

Make Unleavened Bread

*Help your student make unleavened bread, much like the bread that Jesus and other Jewish people of
his day would eat during Passover.*

Ingredients

- 4 c. flour
- 1½ c. water
- Rolling pin
- Fork
- Baking sheet
- Parchment Paper
- (OPTIONAL) 2 Tbsp. olive oil (Adding oil will make the bread softer, a little more like a
  tortilla; not adding oil it will make it more like a cracker)

Directions

1   Tell the student, "In this week's lesson, Jesus and his disciples ate a meal called the Pass-
    over meal. At this meal, all Jewish people were supposed to eat bread made without
    yeast, called 'unleavened bread.' Without the yeast, the bread is flatter and harder than
    most of the bread you are used to eating. It doesn't take long to make. This was to remind
    the Jewish people of the time when they had to leave Egypt in a hurry. Today we're going
    to try making our own unleavened bread."

2   Have the student help you combine the ingredients and knead them for ten minutes, until
    the dough is elastic and shiny.

3   Roll the dough into a ball, cut it in half, and divide each half into 8 pieces.

4   Let the student help you roll out each piece as thinly as possible into oval shapes. You
    should have 16 thin pieces.

5   Pierce each piece with a fork several times. Place them on a baking sheet covered with
    parchment paper. Bake them at 450 to 500 degrees for about 5 minutes, or until slightly
    browned.

Memory Work

John 3:16

This week, as the lessons move toward the culmination of Jesus' mission, the student will memorize John 3:16. Next week she will add John 3:17.

Materials

- John 3:16 (Student Page 293)

Directions

1 Tear out John 3:16 (Student Page 293). Point to the phrases on this page as you learn them in the steps below.

2 Tell the student, "Today we're going to learn something that Jesus said about his mission on earth. He said that he was the Son of God, sent to save the world. This was because God loves the world even though we forget about God and don't obey him."

3 Say, "Repeat this phrase after me three times: 'For God so loved the world . . .'" *[Student says three times: For God so loved the world]*

4 Say, "Now let's add the next line, to find out what God did. Say this after me three times: 'that he gave his one and only Son.'" *[Student says three times: that he gave his one and only Son]*

5 Say, "Let's put that together with the first line. Say this twice: 'For God so loved the world that he gave his one and only Son'" *[Student says twice: For God so loved the world that he gave his one and only Son]*

6 Say, "Now let's add the next line: 'That whoever believes in him should not perish.' Say that with me three times." *[Say together three times: That whoever believes in him should not perish]*

7 Say, "What will happen for people who believe in God's Son? They will have eternal life—life with God, that doesn't go away. Let's say this last line three times together: 'But have eternal life.'" *[Say together three times: But have eternal life.]*

8 Say, "Now let's say the whole thing together: 'For God so loved the world, that he gave his one and only Son, that whoever believes in him should not perish but have eternal life.' *[Say the whole verse together. Give any necessary help or prompting to the student.]*

9 Once the student has learned the verse, Say, "This is from the New Testament book of John, chapter 3, verse 16. You can say 'John three sixteen' after you say the verse, so people who hear you say it will know where in the Bible they can find it for themselves."

10 Use the Student Page as a memory aid over the next few days, to help the student review this verse.

The Last Supper

When Jesus and his disciples ate their last meal together before Jesus was arrested, Jesus told them what was going to happen soon. He was going to die to set people free from sin. He also told the disciples that one of them would hand Jesus over to bad people who wanted to kill him.

John 3:16

For God so loved the world, that he gave his one and only Son, that whoever believes in him should not perish but have eternal life.

Matthew 26:17–28
The Last Supper

Lesson 35: Jesus Suffers and Prays Alone

Activities

Put It Into Practice Activity: **Ask God for Help Doing Something Hard**
Put It Into Practice Activity: **Support a Loved One Through a Difficult Time**
Game (Group or Individual): **The Big Picture**
History Activity: **Uses of Olive Oil**
Memory Work: **John 3:16 and 17**
Coloring Page: **Jesus Prays Alone**

Put It Into Practice Activity

. . . .

Ask God for Help Doing Something Hard

Directions

1 After reading the passage, talk with the student about how Jesus went to God, his Father, in prayer, when he was feeling overwhelmed about what he had to do next. He was sad and he wished he didn't have to do it, but he knew he did. More than anything, he wanted to follow his Father's plan, even though it was really, really hard. So Jesus asked God to make his plan happen.

2 Brainstorm with the student some things that she has to do that are scary or difficult. Perhaps she has the chore of emptying waste baskets around the house, but is scared of collecting the trash from the one in the dark basement. Or, it can be very challenging to use kind words with a sibling, instead of violence or harsh words, but it is the right thing to do. Maybe the concept of "yielding" (like submitting), and letting a sibling take a turn first, is difficult for the student. Ask her how these things are hard or scary to do.

3 Pray together to God the Father, asking for help to do the right thing. For example, "Dear Father in Heaven, please send your strength to Amy when she and Jonathan are arguing. Fill her with your kind and loving Spirit, so that she can take a deep breath and speak gently with her brother. Help her not to panic and try to grab for what she wants, but to remember that you will help us work it out in a peaceful way. We pray in Jesus' Name, Amen."

Put It Into Practice Activity

Support a Loved One through a Difficult Time

Directions

1 Say to the student, "When Jesus went to pray before his crucifixion he asked his friends to keep him company. Everyone needs company sometimes, especially during difficult times."
2 Help your student think of a friend or relative who may be going through a tough time. It could be someone whose parents are getting divorced, maybe someone whose grandparent or relative has died, a sick friend, a child who has been being bullied at school, a friend who has recently lost a pet, etc. Help your student think of things she can do to help and encourage this friend, to help him or her feel supported instead of alone? [Suggestions: Help the student make a card, color a picture, bake some cookies, go to visit the friend to spend some time together, have the friend over to visit, invite the friend to church or call the friend on the phone.]
3 Encourage the student to reach out to others, and it may become a lifelong habit.

Game (Group or Individual)

The Big Picture

Materials

- The Big Picture (Student Page 303) and The Big Picture Answer Key (Student Page 305)
- Pencil

Directions

1 Tear out Student Page 303.
2 Say to the student, "The disciples didn't understand what Jesus was about to do. They did not see the big picture of his plan. They only understood a little part of it."
3 Tell the student that she will be given a page of images. Explain to the student that the images she sees are small, close-up images of larger objects. Without looking at the Answer Page, the student must look at each image and try to identify the object in the image, based on the shapes she sees.
4 Tell the student to write down, on the blanks below the images, what she thinks the object in the picture is. If you are using this activity with a group of students, pick several students to guess the object for each of the images OR show each student one image at a time and have each student write down their guess on a separate sheet of paper.
5 When the student has written down a guess for each of the images, reveal the answers from the answer key below for each image, one at a time.
6 Again, tell the student, "The disciples didn't understand what Jesus was about to do. They did not see the big picture of his plan."

Uses of Olive Oil

Directions

1 Say to the student, "Remember, this week's lesson told us that Jesus prayed in an olive grove called Gethsemane. Gethsemane means 'Oil press'; people would press oil out of olives there, to use for lots of different things."

2 From the list below of the many things olive oil was used for, pick one or a few with your student and use olive oil in these ways for yourselves.

   - For baking and cooking (The Olive Oil Source (www.oliveoilsource.com) has lots of recipes built around using olive oil as well as other useful information about olive oil.)
   - As a spread on bread (Infused olive oil recipes can be found at www.allrecipes.com for use in bread dipping.)
   - Gifts (Infused olive oil and a decorative glass bottle with a cork and ties with a ribbon make wonderful gifts as does olive oil based soap.)
   - Fuel for lamps (Olive Oil lamps can be purchased, as olive oil does burn. Or you can make your own http://www.motherearthnews.com/Do-It-Yourself/Make-Olive-Oil-Lamp.aspx)
   - For anointing (Many churches use oil for pronouncing blessings on people. Ask your priest or pastor if this is something your church does.)

John 3:16 and 17

Materials

- John 3:16 and 17 (Student Page 307)
- (Optional) Crayons, colored pencils, or markers

Directions

1 Tear out John 3:16 and 17 (Student Page 307). Point to the phrases on that page as you introduce them in the steps below.

2 Say to the student, "Last week we learned John 3:16. Let's say that together now." *[Say together: For God so loved the world, that he gave his one and only Son, that whoever believes in him should not perish but have eternal life.]*

3 Say, "This week we will learn what the next verse, John 3:17, says. It tells us more about God's Son, Jesus. He didn't come to punish people but to rescue them. Say this first part after me, three times: 'For God did not send his Son into the world to condemn the world.'" *[Student says three times: For God did not send his Son into the world to condemn*

the world.]

4   Say, "Now say this last line three times: 'but to save the world through him.'" *[Student says three times: but to save the world through him.]*

5   Say, "Good job. Now let's put that verse together. Say it with me twice." *[Say together: For God did not send his Son into the world to condemn the world, but to save the world through him.]*

6   Say, "And now let's put it all together with the verse we learned last week, John 3:16. Let's say the whole thing together." *[Say together, giving any necessary prompting to the student: For God so loved the world, that he gave his one and only Son, that whoever believes in him should not perish but have eternal life. For God did not send his Son into the world to condemn the world, but to save the world through him."]*

7   If the student desires, allow her to decorate the Student Page (perhaps with a picture of the world that God loves). Use the Student page to review these verses in the coming week.

Coloring Page

Jesus Prays Alone

Jesus knew that he was about to be captured and killed, and he was very sad. He asked his friends to stay with him and pray, but they all fell asleep. He prayed to God about the hard things he would have to do the next day.

The Big Picture

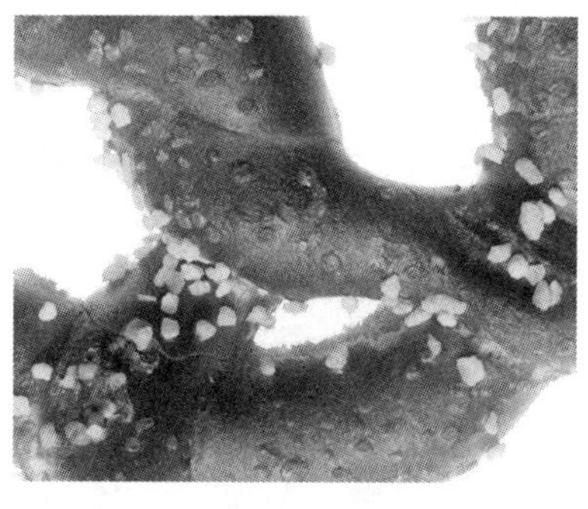

The Big Picture Answer Key

Leaf

Strawberry

Butterfly

Turtle

Barn

Flower

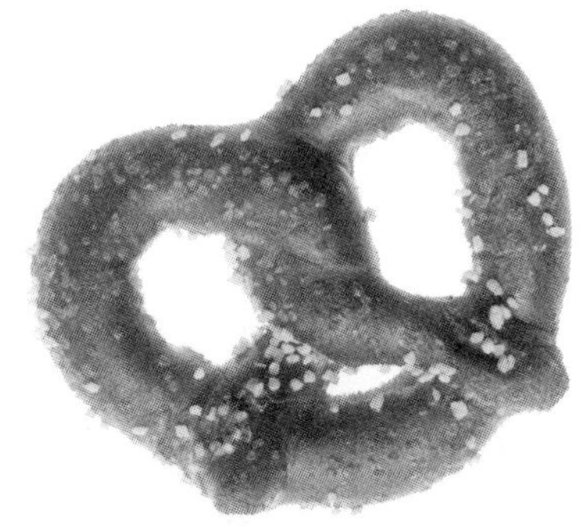

Pretzel

Owl

Fish

John 3:16–17

For God so loved the world, that he gave his one and only Son, that whoever believes in him should not perish but have eternal life. For God did not send his Son into the world to condemn the world, but to save the world through him.

Matthew 26:36-46
Jesus Prays Alone

Lesson 36: Jesus Doesn't Fight Back When Arrested

Activities

Review Activity (Group or Individual): **Betrayal Word Search**
Craft Project (Group or Individual): **Make a Model of Gethsemane**
Craft (Group or Individual): **Angels**
Review Activity: **Tell the Story of Jesus' Arrest**
Coloring Page: **Jesus is Arrested**

Review Activity

Betrayal Word Search

Materials

- Betrayal Word Search (Student Page 317)
- Pencil

Directions

1 Have the student look at the Word Search on Student Page 317.
2 Have the student find key words from this week's story in the word search. The words may be horizontal or vertical, or written diagonally.
3 Use this answer key on the next page to help the student if necessary.

```
S Q I H R D G G H O B J K X C
S I O E T A R H Z E E C O S A
U P G J R E B J Z E Q L D O B
S S P N E T W B Z L J Q X N B
E F W T A Q Z U I A R R E S T
J U I O W L S R I Q J C E D E
D N C M R W L T E A C H E R V
G B F W V D U J L K R F U F L
B Y F C Z S N Q F P J J O I E
E I Z F Y V N X J M A U G Z W
T Z K V S Z B Z C O I N D T T
C O Q G E T H S E M A N E A B
D P D F R I E N D K I S S X S
Y H W R G B T N F Z A C X H I
X Y P K Y E Z F A Q S W Q K V
```

(Over,Down,Direction)
ARREST(10,5,E)
FRIEND(4,13,E)
GETHSEMANE(4,12,E)
GREETING(8,1,SW)
JESUS(1,6,N)
JUDAS(11,9,SE)
KISS(10,13,E)
RABBI(5,1,SE)
SIGNAL(1,1,SE)
SWORD(2,4,SE)
TEACHER(8,7,E)
TWELVE(15,11,N)

Craft Project

• •

Make a Model of Gethsemane

Materials

- Thin cardboard sheet (from a cereal box)
- 2 Paper-towel tubes or 3–4 toilet paper tubes
- Sheet of green construction paper
- Scissors
- Very small plastic or paper disposable cup, with the top half cut off
- Gray crayon or marker or colored pencil
- Scotch tape
- Strips of tree bark
- Toothpicks
- Play-doh
- Chopped-up grass
- Small leaves (including stems)
- Olives
- Glue stick
- Stone about the size of a golf ball
- Few small pebbles
- Lego figures or action figures

Directions

1 Say to the student, "In this week's lesson, Jesus and his disciples went to a hill called the Mount of Olives. They went to a place, on the hill, called Gethsemane [*say* geth SEM ah nee]. Say that word with me: Gethsemane. That word means 'Oil press.' It was a place where olives were grown and then pressed under a heavy stone to squeeze out the olive oil, which was used for cooking and to fuel lamps."

2 Say to the student, "Today we'll make a little model of Gethsemane. This cardboard piece will be the base. The green paper will be our hill."

3 Lay the cardboard sheet onto your work surface. Cut the cardboard tubes in half to shorten them, and place them at the center of the cardboard sheet, forming a mound. This will give your hill its "height." Place the sheet of green construction paper over the tubes, covering the mound, and have the student help you secure the paper to either end of the cardboard base-sheet, using tape.

4 Help the student glue the grass to the construction paper and to the base of the "hill" to form the grassy covering of the hill.

5 To make an olive tree: roll some of the Play-doh between your hands into a "snake" or cylinder shape, for the trunk. Flatten one end, and stick it to the paper at the bottom of the hill (it won't stand up well, if you put it at the top). Press some pieces of bark onto this "trunk" to make it look more tree-like. Stick the leaves into the top of the trunk to create the "leaves and branches" of the tree. Stick olives onto toothpicks and poke those into the trunk too, to create olive-laden branches.

6 To make the olive press: cut off the top half of the disposable cup, color the remaining cup gray, and glue this gray bottom half to the construction paper "ground." Put a few olives inside, and cover it with the large stone.

7 If the student wants to, he can make a path up the hill using the pebbles. The toy people, representing the disciples, could be sleeping at the top of the hill next to the olive press.

Craft

. . . .

Angels

Materials

- Paper
- Drawing supplies (crayons, markers, colored pencils, etc.)
- OPTIONAL: Bible

Directions

1 Tell the student, "Angels are creatures who worship and serve God as messengers. The Bible tells us they sometimes look very frightening and terrifying, as well as beautiful. In the story we read this week, Jesus says that he could summon a whole army of angels to do whatever he wanted. What do you think an army of angels would look like? Draw a picture of that."

2   Let the student draw a picture of an army of angels. [Depending on whether or not you think the student would find this too intense, you could give him some descriptions of angels from Isaiah 6:2, Matthew 28:2–4, or Revelation 4:6–8].

3   When the student is finished, after proper admiring of the picture, tell him "Jesus could have summoned an army of angels just like this to come and save him from the crowd. Instead, he was obedient to God and went with the people who arrested him. He was so powerful he could have commanded all these angels, but he went to die peacefully so that our sins could be forgiven."

Review Activity

Tell the Story of Jesus' Arrest

Materials

- Scissors
- Glue stick
- One sheet of construction paper
- "Tell the Story of Jesus' Arrest" (Student Page 319)

Directions

1   Tear out Student Page 319. Show it to the student and tell him, "These pictures tell the story that we heard in this week's lesson, of how Judas led the soldiers to Jesus so they could capture him. But they aren't in the right order; they are all mixed up. Let's see if we can put them in the right order, to tell the story."

2   Have the student help you cut out each of the seven story panels from Student Page 319.

3   When the panels have all been cut out, spread them out on a table, and have the student try to put them into the correct order. If he has trouble remembering the order of events, use the text of Matthew 26:47—57 (printed below) to remind him what happened.

Matthew 26: 47—57

While he was still speaking, Judas, one of the Twelve, arrived. With him was a large crowd armed with swords and clubs, sent from the chief priests and the elders of the people. Now the betrayer had arranged a signal with them: "The one I kiss is the man; arrest him." Going at once to Jesus, Judas said, "Greetings, Rabbi!" and kissed him.

Jesus replied, "Do what you came for, friend."

Then the men stepped forward, seized Jesus and arrested him. With that, one of Jesus' companions reached for his sword, drew it out and struck the servant of the high priest, cutting off his ear.

"Put your sword back in its place," Jesus said to him, "for all who draw the sword will die by the sword. Do you think I cannot call on my Father, and he will at once put at my disposal more than twelve legions of angels? But how then would the Scriptures be fulfilled that say it must happen in this way?"

In that hour Jesus said to the crowd, "Am I leading a rebellion, that you have come out with swords and clubs to capture me? Every day I sat in the temple courts teaching, and you did not arrest me. But this has all taken place that the writings of the prophets might be fulfilled." Then all the disciples deserted him and fled.

Those who had arrested Jesus took him away to Caiaphas the high priest, where the teachers of the law and the elders had assembled.

The correct order for the panels:
1. Picture of Jesus talking to disciples in the Garden of Gethsemane
2. Soldiers with torches looking for Jesus
3. Judas kisses Jesus, showing the soldiers who to arrest
4. One of the disciples uses a sword to strike one of the arresting soldiers on the ear
5. Jesus rebukes the disciple and orders him to put away the sword
6. Jesus heals the man's ear
7. The soldiers lead Jesus away

4 Once the panels are in the correct order, have the student use the glue stick to glue the panels to the construction paper.

Coloring Page

Jesus is Arrested

The leaders who hated Jesus sent a crowd of their servants and soldiers to arrest him. One of his disciples, Judas, showed them who Jesus was so that they knew who to capture. Jesus did not fight against the crowd. He went with them, to carry out God's great plan.

Betrayal Word Search

```
S  Q  I  H  R  D  G  G  H  O  B  J  K  X  C
S  I  O  E  T  A  R  H  Z  E  E  C  O  S  A
U  P  G  J  R  E  B  J  Z  E  Q  L  D  O  B
S  S  P  N  E  T  W  B  Z  L  J  Q  X  N  B
E  F  W  T  A  Q  Z  U  I  A  R  R  E  S  T
J  U  I  O  W  L  S  R  I  Q  J  C  E  D  E
D  N  C  M  R  W  L  T  E  A  C  H  E  R  V
G  B  F  W  V  D  U  J  L  K  R  F  U  F  L
B  Y  F  C  Z  S  N  Q  F  P  J  J  O  I  E
E  I  Z  F  Y  V  N  X  J  M  A  U  G  Z  W
T  Z  K  V  S  Z  B  Z  C  O  I  N  D  T  T
C  O  Q  G  E  T  H  S  E  M  A  N  E  A  B
D  P  D  F  R  I  E  N  D  K  I  S  S  X  S
Y  H  W  R  G  B  T  N  F  Z  A  C  X  H  I
X  Y  P  K  Y  E  Z  F  A  Q  S  W  Q  K  V
```

ARREST	FRIEND	GETHSEMANE
GREETING	JESUS	JUDAS
KISS	RABBI	SIGNAL
SWORD	TEACHER	TWELVE

Tell the Story of Jesus' Arrest

Matthew 26:47-56
Jesus is Arrested

The Rest of the Story

Supplemental Lesson 1: A Politician Condemns an Innocent Man

Activities

Craft Project: The Royal Robe of Tyrian Purple
Art Project: *Ecce Homo* Viewing Box
Coloring Page: Pilate's Men Make Fun of Jesus

Craft Project

• •

The Royal Robe of Tyrian Purple

After Pilate had Jesus flogged, he mocked him by placing a crown of thorns on his head and dressing him in a purple robe. This project teaches why royal robes were purple and how the color "Tyrian purple" was made, and lets the student experiment with making her own natural dyes for cloth.

Materials

- Large stainless steel pot
- Wet and dry cup measures
- Water
- Rubber gloves
- White cloth item to be dyed, such as a T-shirt or pillowcase [To experiment with plant dyes, use scraps from a T-shirt or sheet (natural fibers like cotton, wool, & linen work best).]
- 7 oz. of a dye source (choose only one plant)

Pink	Green	Brown/Yellow
Strawberries	Spinach	Black tea leaves
Cherries	Kale	Onion skins
Red roses	Swiss chard	Dandelion flowers

- OPTIONAL: 2 oz. (⅓ c.) alum powder (This helps fabric absorb dye well. You can find it in the spice aisle of a grocery store.)

Directions

1 Tell the student, "After Pilate had Jesus beaten and flogged, he dressed him up as a mock king with a crown and a royal robe. The robe was purple. Purple was the color worn by royalty: kings and queens. Can you guess why purple was the color that kings wore?"

2 Tell the student, "Kings and queens wore purple because purple cloth was the most expensive. It cost so much because it took so much time to dye cloth that color. Wool, linen, and silk are naturally pale in color—if you wanted cloth to be a vibrant color, you had to dye the cloth by staining it with something that would not wash out. Most dyes were made from boiling the leaves, berries, or roots of plants. But the color of purple, called Tyrian purple, was not made from plants. Can you guess how the purple dye was made? Here's a hint: Tyre is a country by the sea." Give the student a chance to guess.

3 Tell the student, "The purple dye came from sea snails! Sea snails eat other shelled creatures, and they use the purple liquid to help pierce through the shells of their prey. Dye-makers collected thousands of snails, crushed them, and put them in a huge vat of boiling water. The water boiled for days and the color of the water would get darker and darker. Then it was time to dip the fabric into the water—and when it came out it was purple! It took over ten thousand sea snails to make even the tiniest amount of purple dye."

4 It is now time to have the student make her own dye. If you do not have alum powder, go on to step 5. If you have alum powder, have the student put 2 ounces (⅓ c.) into the stainless steel pot and add 4 cups of water. Bring to a boil and add the white fabric. Let it simmer for 45 minutes. Let the water cool. Then let the student rinse the fabric in cool water. Now go on to step 5.

5 Have the student put 7 ounces of your dye source into the empty stainless steel pot. Add 11 cups of water. Bring to a boil. Add the cloth. Let the mixture simmer for 45 minutes or until the cloth is the color you want.

6 Carefully remove the cloth and place it in a bowl or the sink to let it cool. Once the cloth is cool, have the student put on the rubber gloves and wring out the cloth. Let dry. NOTE: Plant dye is not colorfast, so wash this item separately from other clothing!

Art Project

· ·

Ecce Homo Viewing Box

Ecce Homo [say EH chay HOH moh], Latin for "Behold the Man," is the Latin translation of the words Pilate pronounces as he shows Jesus to the angry crowd. Many artists have painted this scene: Jesus with a crown of thorns and a purple robe (perhaps with Pilate standing near). Let the student see several depictions of this scene by famous artists, and then let her draw her own version (or use the coloring page) to create an Ecce Homo *viewing box.*

Materials

- Computer with Internet access
- Plain white paper for original art (or "Behold the Man" image on Student Page 327)
- Art supplies (crayons, markers, paint, or pastels, etc.)
- Ruler
- Scissors

- Black construction paper
- Scotch tape
- 1 sheet construction paper, any color but black
- Glue stick
- Flashlight
- Shoebox

Directions

1. Before your time with the student, go online and pick out a few *Ecce Homo* paintings you would like to show the student (choose ones you think are suitable/appropriate, as this can be a grim scene). Here are some suggestions that you can put into any image search engine: *Ecce Homo* by Caravaggio, Titian, Antonio Ciseri, Bosch, Rembrandt, Correggio and Andrea Solari.

2. Tell the student that this scene has been painted by many artists. Show the student the paintings and tell her that *Ecce Homo* means "Behold the Man." Point out, using the painting, that after Pilate had Jesus beaten and flogged, he dressed him mockingly as a king: a purple robe, a crown of thorns, and a reed to hold as a scepter.

3. Measure the small rectangular end of the shoebox. Cut a piece of plain white paper that size if the student wishes to do her own version of *Ecce Homo*. Or you can use the scaled-down version of our coloring page on Student Page 327.

4. If the student chooses to color the coloring page, have her do so. If the student is doing her own composition, she may choose to include or exclude Pilate.

5. Have the student tape the finished colored page to the inside of the shoebox (tape it to the inside of the small rectangular end).

6. Put the lid on the shoebox and tape it closed. Use the scissors to poke a hole in the end of the shoebox opposite the picture (so you can look through the hole to see the picture). Also poke a small hole in the underside of the shoebox, near the end where the *Ecce Homo* picture sits. This hole will be for the light source.

7. Have the student wrap the outside of the shoebox with black paper and glue it to the shoebox. Use the scissors to poke holes through the paper where the two holes in the cardboard are.

8. Have the student print "Ecce Homo" in block letters on the colored paper. Cut out the letters with scissors and glue them to the top of the shoe box.

9. Now the viewing box is complete! Hold a flashlight up to the hole on the box's underside and look through the viewing hole to "Behold the Man."

Coloring Page

· ·

Pilate Lets Jesus Be Mocked

The Roman governor, Pontius Pilate, didn't really believe that Jesus was a king. So he let his men make fun of Jesus. They made him wear a royal robe and a crown of thorns, and they hit him. Pilate said that the crowd could have its way, and Jesus could be killed. He didn't treat Jesus fairly, as he should have. (This picture is based on a painting by Antonio Ciseri.)

"Behold the Man" image

John 19:1–16
Pilate Lets Jesus Be Mocked

Supplemental Lesson 2: The Death of Jesus Fulfills Scripture

Activities

Cooking Activity: **Make Flavored Vinegar**
Activity: **"Jesus' Death Fulfills Scripture" Match-Up**
Music Activity: **O *Sacred Head, Now Wounded***
Coloring Page: **Vinegar and Hyssop**

Cooking Activity

. . . .

Make Flavored Vinegar

Jesus was offered a sponge soaked in vinegar. The process of making actual vinegar takes months, but this project teaches how wine vinegar is made and lets the student experiment with making his own vinegar flavored with fruit or herbs.

Materials

- A glass jar or bottle with a tight-fitting lid [Note: There should be no metal touching the vinegar. You can use a mason jar or pickle jar with a metal lid; just cover the top with a layer of plastic wrap before you screw the lid in place.]
- White vinegar (enough to fill the jar)
- Saucepan
- A flavoring (choose one; you'll need enough of the flavoring to fill the jar about halfway):
    - Fresh herbs still on the stalk such as oregano, thyme, rosemary
    - Peeled garlic cloves
    - Any citrus rinds
    - Fresh berries like strawberries, blueberries, or raspberries
- A funnel (optional, but helpful if your jar has a narrow mouth)
- Fine-mesh strainer or cheesecloth

Directions

1 Gently boil the jar and lid in a pan full of water for 10 minutes.
2 After the student has chosen which ingredient he will use as a flavoring, have him wash

that ingredient thoroughly. While he washes, tell him that he will be adding flavor to vinegar that is already made. In Jesus' day, people would make vinegar by letting wine sit out for months. Bacteria would eat the alcohol in the wine and turn the alcohol into acetic acid that gives vinegar its taste. This process is called fermentation. Let the student put a dab of vinegar on his tongue and ask him how it tastes (sour!).

3 Remove the jar and lid from the water. Let cool. Dry off.

4 Let the student add the flavoring to the jar. Fill the jar about halfway.

5 Help the student pour in the vinegar to the top of the jar (use a funnel to make this a neater process). Secure with a lid (use a layer of plastic wrap if the lid is metal).

6 The student should shake the jar. Put the flavored vinegar in the refrigerator.

7 Every day for the next two weeks, have the student shake the jar of vinegar.

8 After two weeks, have the student put the fine-mesh strainer or cheesecloth over a bowl and pour in the flavored vinegar. Discard the flavoring in the strainer.

9 Wash the glass jar and lid, and then pour the vinegar back into the jar. Secure the lid and store in the refrigerator for up to three months.

10 Use your flavored vinegar in salad dressings (1 part vinegar to two parts oil plus salt and pepper), meat marinades (1 cup vinegar, 3 tsp. sugar, plus desired herbs and spices), or drizzle it over cooked vegctables.

Activity

Jesus' Death Fulfills Scripture Match-Up

This activity directs the student to the Old Testament prophecies about Jesus' death and helps the student make connections about how those prophecies were fulfilled.

Materials

- Jesus' Death Fulfills Scripture (Student Page 335)
- Pencil
- Bible

Directions

1 Help the student, as necessary, to look up each Bible verse listed on the worksheet, read it aloud, and draw a line to how it was fulfilled in the death of Jesus. (If the student is not yet a confident reader, you may read the verse aloud to him.)

2 Answer Key: 1 C, 2 A, 3 D, 4 B

Music Activity

O Sacred Head, Now Wounded

Read the lyrics and listen to this famous Passion hymn, whose words were composed in the Middle Ages and whose music was harmonized by Bach.

Materials

- "O Sacred Head, Now Wounded" Lyrics Sheet (Student Page 337)
- Computer with Internet access

Directions

1   Look at the lyrics sheet (Student Page 337) with the student. Tell the student, "These are the words to a hymn that is sung in many churches around Easter time. The words are from a long poem in Latin that was written over 800 years ago. The original poem is longer, but today we'll learn the part that most churches sing today."

2   Tell the student about how the Latin poem became a hymn: "About 400 years ago a German hymn writer named Paul Gerhardt translated the words of the poem into German and the hymn was set it to the tune of a popular love song." Listen to the tune on Youtube.com by searching for "O Sacred Head, Now Wounded" and selecting one that is instrumental. The composer J. S. Bach added his own harmonies to the hymn and put it in his work called *St. Matthew Passion,* which tells the story of Christ's death through song.

3   Say to the student, "Now I'll read you the English version of the words to this hymn." [The most common version is from a translation by J. W. Alexander in the early 1800s. This translation is on the student page.] Read the lyrics on Student Page 337 to the student. Talk about the meaning of the words (you will probably need to tell the student that "visage" refers to a person's face or appearance).

4   Listen to the song sung with lyrics, on Youtube.com (the Choir of King's College does a beautiful choral version, and Fernando Ortega performs the piece as a solo with piano accompaniment). Some arrangements use other English translations. Before you listen to the piece, tell the student to listen for the part in the first verse of the hymn that talks about what the soldiers did to Jesus. Ask, "The hymn says that the soldiers put something on Jesus' head. What was it?" (Answer: *They put a crown of thorns on his head.*)

Coloring Page

• •

Vinegar and Hyssop

When Jesus was on the cross, he was very thirsty. Someone put wine vinegar on a sponge, and used a hyssop branch to lift it up to him so he could drink. In one of the psalms from the Old Testament, the writer of the psalm, David, is suffering because he is being attacked by his enemies. He is totally exhausted and in one verse he says, "My tongue sticks to the roof of my mouth." Jesus was parched with thirst, too; the psalm is not just talking about David's suffering but Jesus' also.

Jesus' Death Fulfills Scripture

1) Psalm 22: 15

2) Psalm 69: 21

3) Numbers 9: 12

4) Zechariah 12: 10

A. Jesus is given vinegar to drink.

B. Jesus' side is pierced with a spear.

C. Jesus is extremely thirsty.

D. Like the lamb killed at Passover, Jesus' bones are not broken.

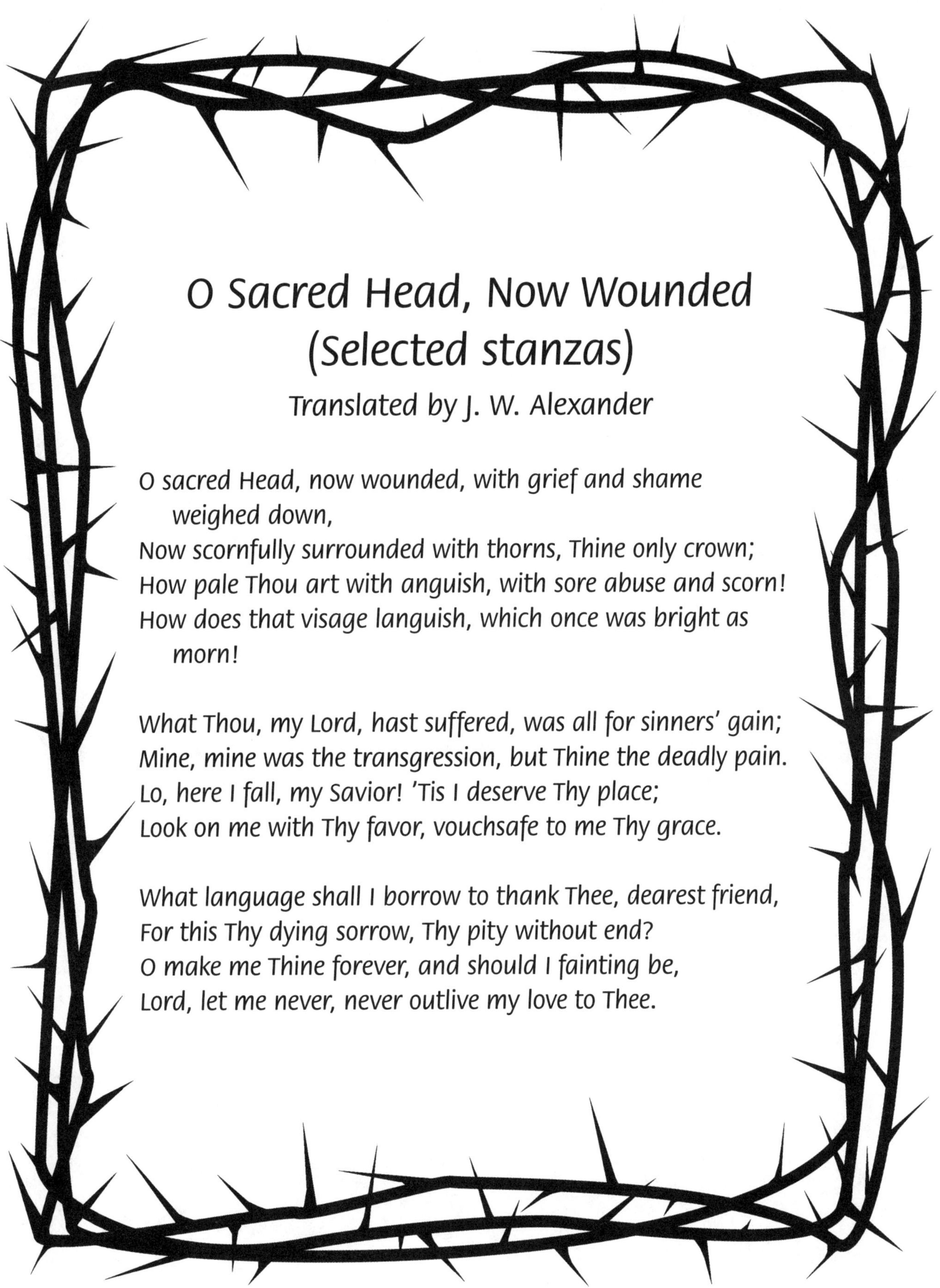

O Sacred Head, Now Wounded
(Selected stanzas)
Translated by J. W. Alexander

O sacred Head, now wounded, with grief and shame
  weighed down,
Now scornfully surrounded with thorns, Thine only crown;
How pale Thou art with anguish, with sore abuse and scorn!
How does that visage languish, which once was bright as
  morn!

What Thou, my Lord, hast suffered, was all for sinners' gain;
Mine, mine was the transgression, but Thine the deadly pain.
Lo, here I fall, my Savior! 'Tis I deserve Thy place;
Look on me with Thy favor, vouchsafe to me Thy grace.

What language shall I borrow to thank Thee, dearest friend,
For this Thy dying sorrow, Thy pity without end?
O make me Thine forever, and should I fainting be,
Lord, let me never, never outlive my love to Thee.

John 19:28–37
They Gave Jesus Vinegar to Drink, on a Sponge

Supplemental Lesson 3:
Mary Magdalene Spreads the News That Jesus is Alive

Activities

Review Activity: **Jesus Meets Mary Magdalene Word Search**
Craft Project: **Create a Garden Collage**
Group Game: **Spread the News (in Four Languages)**
Coloring Page: **Mary Magdalene Sees Jesus**

Review Activity

Jesus Meets Mary Magdalene Word Search

Materials

- Jesus Meets Mary Magdalene Word Search (Student Page 345) and John 20:10–18 (Student Page 347)
- Pencil

Directions

1 Tear out Student Page 345, containing the Jesus Meets Mary Magdalene Word Search, and Student Page 347, containing John 20:10–18, the passage from this week's lesson.
2 Have the student look at the Word Search on Student Page 345. Reread the Bible passage from the lesson, John 20:10–18, from its Student Page. Point out the words in bold.
3 Have the student find the bolded words in the word search. The words may be horizontal or vertical, forward or backward.

Answer Key:

M	R	A	B	B	O	N	I	P	R	F
K	C	N	K	E	W	O	M	A	N	J
J	V	G	A	R	D	E	N	E	R	E
H	O	E	L	E	I	B	I	I	T	S
G	B	L	F	K	S	T	X	U	E	U
N	Z	S	A	Y	C	H	I	P	A	S
I	M	O	T	E	I	R	M	E	C	Q
Y	N	T	H	L	P	E	A	I	H	O
R	R	S	E	S	L	O	R	D	E	H
C	P	Q	R	K	E	P	Y	U	R	R
D	O	N	G	A	S	E	T	O	M	B

Create a Garden Collage

Use magazines, scissors, and glue to make a vibrant garden collage, and learn about some native plants from first century Palestine.

Materials

- Seed catalogs and/or garden magazines
- Scissors
- Glue stick
- Piece of blank paper

Directions

1 Have the student go through the seed catalogs and garden magazines and clip out pictures of trees, plants, and flowers that she likes. Here are some plants that could have been found in a garden from first-century Palestine. If the student finds any of these, cut them out (here is where a seed catalog index comes in handy!):

> Olive tree
> Poplar tree
> Lupines
> Morning glories
> Cornflowers
> Anemones

2 Have the student trim the edges of the pictures. She should then arrange them on the blank piece of paper. Once she is happy with the arrangement, have the student use the glue stick to secure the clippings in place.

Spread the News

Many churches use an Easter greeting and response, to celebrate Christ's resurrection. A leader says "Christ has risen!" and the people respond, "He has risen, indeed!" or "Indeed, he has risen!" This group game will teach your students the Resurrection greeting and response in four languages used in Orthodox churches, and will put their knowledge to the test with a game of tag.

Materials

- Timer
  [Because the Orthodox Church exists all over the world and in America is made up of several different cultures, the Orthodox greeting is said in many different languages. In churches in America it will be said in English, and then in the language that the church was founded under (often Russian, Greek or Arabic). Then the priest will often say the greeting in any of the traditional or ancestral languages of the members of the congregations. It requires a lot of practice and memorization for the priest as he may say "Christ is Risen" in up to 15 languages at the Pascha [Easter] service! http://www.youtube.com/watch?v=cNScQj7BTbg In a Pascha service the whole congregation says, shouts, and sings the greeting over 50 times.]

Directions

Note to Instructor: This game is a modified version of freeze tag. There is an easy version, an intermediate version, and an advanced version. All three versions use the Resurrection greetings in various languages, so first, practice these greetings with the students.
English: Christ is risen! Indeed He is risen!
Greek: Christos anesti! Alithos anesti! (KREES-tos ah-NES-tee) and (ah-lee-THOHSS ah-NES-tee)
Russian: Khristos voskrese! Voistinu voskrese! (KREES-tos vos -krees-eh) and (Voiz-te-noh vos -KREES-eh)
Arabic: El Messieh kahm! Hakken kahm! (El Mes-EE KHAM- a) and (HAWK-en KHAM-a)

Easy Version

1. You will play four rounds, one for each language. Start with English and then progress into the harder languages. Before each round begins, help the students practice the greeting again in the language you are going to use for that round.
2. Decide how long you want a round to go on and then set a timer.
3. Pick someone to be "it," the tagger, first. Tell the tagger that she must try to tag the other students. In order to tag the other students, she needs to tag them *and also* say the first part of the greeting ("Christ is risen!"). If the tagger can remember the first part of the greeting and tags a student, that student is now "frozen" and cannot move.
4. There are two ways for a frozen student to become un-frozen. The first and easiest is to simply be able to say aloud the response to the greeting ("Indeed he is risen!") in the language in which the greeting was said. If the student cannot remember the response, then one of the other students running from the tagger can touch the frozen student and say the response for them.

1   In this version, you will play one round, with four taggers instead of one. Each of the four taggers needs to remember the first part of the greeting in just one language; the tag-ees need to remember the responses in all four languages. Each tagger is assigned a language (Russian, Greek, English, or Arabic).
2   Decide how long you want a round to go on and then set a timer.
3   Instruct the taggers to tag the other students and say the first part of the greeting in their assigned language as they tag them.
4   Once a student has been tagged, there are two ways for her to get un-frozen. The first and easiest is to simply say aloud the response, in the same language that she was tagged in (Greek for Greek, Russian for Russian, etc). If the student cannot remember the proper response, then it is up to one of the other students running from the taggers to touch the frozen student and say the response for them (in the language that the student was tagged in).

Advanced Version

1   In this version, you will use with one tagger at a time. The tagger needs to remember the first part of all four greetings. The tag-ees need to remember the responses in all four languages.
2   Instruct the tagger to try and tag the other students and say the first part of the greeting in any language they choose as they tag them (you may want to take using English out of the game if it is over-used!)
3   There are two ways to for the students to get un-frozen. The first and easiest is to simply be able to say aloud the return part of the greeting, in the same language that the tagger choose. If the student cannot remember the part of the greeting then it is up to one of the other students running from "it" to touch the frozen student and say the response (in the language that the student was tagged in) for them. The tagger will not be able to tag everyone or keep everyone tagged, so decide how long you want a round to go on and then set a timer.

If your family, or a student in your class has an ancestral or traditional language that you want to use as well, you can find the greeting in many different languages here: http://www.oca.org/ocpaschalgreetings.asp?sid=2

Coloring Page
• •
Mary Magdalene Sees Jesus

Mary Magdalene, one of Jesus' followers, was sad because she thought someone had taken away his dead body. Then she saw Jesus and heard him say her name, and she realized that he was alive again! He told her to go tell the disciples that he was alive.

Jesus Meets Mary Magdalene
Word Search

```
M  R  A  B  B  O  N  I  P  R  F
K  C  N  K  E  W  O  M  A  N  J
J  V  G  A  R  D  E  N  E  R  E
H  O  E  L  E  I  B  I  I  T  S
G  B  L  F  K  S  T  X  U  E  U
N  Z  S  A  Y  C  H  I  P  A  S
I  M  O  T  E  I  R  M  E  C  Q
Y  N  T  H  L  P  E  A  I  H  O
R  R  S  E  S  L  O  R  D  E  H
C  P  Q  R  K  E  P  Y  U  R  R
D  O  N  G  A  S  E  T  O  M  B
```

Jesus Meets Mary Magdalene
Word Search: John 20:10–18

On the Word Search page, find the words that are bolded in this Bible story.

Then the **disciples** went back to their homes, but **Mary** stood outside the tomb crying. As she wept, she bent over to look into the **tomb** and saw two **angels** in white, seated where Jesus' body had been, one at the head and the other at the foot.

They asked her, "Woman, why are you **crying**?"

"They have taken my Lord away," she said, "and I don't know where they have put him." At this, she turned around and saw Jesus standing there, but she did not realize that it was **Jesus**.

"**Woman**," he said, "why are you **crying**? Who is it you are looking for?"

Thinking he was the **gardener**, she said, "Sir, if you have carried him away, tell me where you have put him, and I will get him."

Jesus said to her, "Mary."

She turned toward him and cried out in Aramaic, "**Rabboni**!" (which means **Teacher**).

Jesus said, "Do not hold on to me, for I have not yet returned to the **Father**. Go instead to my brothers and tell them, 'I am returning to my Father and your Father, to my God and your God.' "

Mary Magdalene went to the disciples with the news: "I have seen the **Lord**!" And she told them that he had said these things to her.

John 20:10–18
Mary Magdalene Finds Out That Jesus is Alive!